NORSE PAGANISM

A Modern Beginner's Guide to Asatru &
Heathenry, their Gods, Rituals, and
Ceremonies to Understanding the Mysteries of
the Northern Traditions

By Hans Niklas Hellström

OrangePen Publications is a company of writers, designers, editors,researchers and other professionals, who have formed a team to create and publish unique and extraordinary works of literature. The main purpose of **OrangePen Publications** is to spread information and help people improve their lives thanks to indepth, comprehensive communication, resulting from years of study and research. The publications cover many areas of life - health, psychology, investing, relationships, spirituality, and more - and each area has its own author. Quality literature and customer satisfaction are primary aspects of our work, which is why the **OrangePen Publications** team continually seeks out new topics to provide content-rich, in-depth reading.

Table of Contents

Introduction

Norse magic is hugely influenced by the concept of fate, whether concerning a person's destiny or affecting it. Its practitioners view it as a way to examine and perhaps exert some control over their fate, but it is not used to change it. Norse magic is also devoted to the idea of being able to manifest our desires. Once you learn how mysterious Norse magic is, it should come as no surprise that the word "rune" itself means mystery, whisper, or secret. We are starting as beginners, but there's no better place or time than this to bring the power of Norse magic into our lives.

For magic to exist, the gods must struggle against one another—they're the only beings powerful enough to manipulate the power of runes. One of the best characteristics of Asatru is that it is a great private religion. You can be an Asatruar, and no one else needs to know about your beliefs but you. You are free to choose what attracts you to Asatru. And yet, numerous kindred groups all over the world offer you a sense of identity and connection with other practicing Asatruars. Later in the book, you'll discover how to contact practitioners in your area and even learn how to start your hearth.

This book contains that kind of information too, such as how to practice Asatru on your own, as well as how to find other practitioners and be part of a similar group. The hands-on instructions on how to practice this belief system at home will give you sufficient material to start immediately, even as you prepare yourself to become part of something larger. Some magic is based on beings that are seen more as spirits and less as deities.

Norse magic believes that everything in this world has a spiritual connection, both good and bad. There are many ways to practice it, and this guide will learn some of the most common methods. Both rune magic and seidhr are reliant on the Norse gods for their power.

You may find them enchanting for their unique and often cryptic nature, or you may wish to practice divination with them. You can just experiment and see which runes are proper for you.

Norse magic in your life can take many forms. It might be as simple as casting a simple spell, or it could be a complex ritual of runes and pagan beliefs. One thing is for sure, though — magic gives your life and soul purpose and substance.

It is an activity with no strings attached but it's still quite special and unique in its own right. The search isn't easy, as many requisites must go right before the magic can be used effectively.

Many people can tap into the power of magic, but only an elite few are successful at it. The key is to breathe life into your craft and ask your gods for guidance. Your magic will reveal itself eventually, but only after you learn how to make it happen.

Chapter 1: The Origins and History of Norse Religion

A Brief History of the Norseman

The Norse people, commonly known as Vikings, were seafaring warlords and warriors from pagan Scandinavia. They had such a great impact on Europe's history that the time in which they raided, colonized, and conquered European soils, from around the ninth to the 11th century, was named after them: "the Viking Age." When we hear the word "Vikings," we can't help but imagine an army of barbarians who bowed to no gods and who only took pleasure in plundering and raiding. Honestly, we are not to blame for having this mental image. That's just how Vikings are usually portrayed, and the concept is stuck somewhere deep in our subconscious mind. But is this image close to the historical truth?

Vikings came from Sweden, Norway, and Denmark, many hundreds of years before they were recognized as stand-alone countries, and they were mostly land-owning farmers and fishermen. They lived in villages ruled by chieftains or clan leaders, and they had few towns. Chieftains often fought for dominance over the lands, and with a seemingly inexhaustible arsenal of strong men who sought adventure, it was fairly easy for skillful leaders to organize armies and fearful bands. Historians are unsure what prompted Vikings to leave their lands and become seafaring pillagers, but they do propose a couple of theories.

The political instability caused by the frequent clashes between clans makes a good motive for branching out. Another would be localized overpopulation, which led to families owning smaller and smaller lands that could no longer provide sustenance for all the family members. Additionally, around the seventh and eighth centuries, the Vikings refined the way they constructed ships and vessels, adding sails and modifying their structures to sustain longer voyages. These longships were swift and shallow, allowing them to go across the North Sea and land on the beaches of unsuspecting lands. If we consider shipping advances, the troubled socio-economic situation of the Vikings at the time, the adventurous nature of these warrior-spirited people, and the tales of riches brought along by merchants, it's not hard to understand why one day they decided to raid the coasts of Europe.

The writers and chronicles of the Viking Era had no qualms when it came to demonizing and denigrating the Scandinavian people who ravaged their land. Clerics, such as Alcuin of York, were especially dramatic in their account of Viking raids on monasteries and places of worship, describing the carnage in minute detail and painting the assailants as demonic beasts rather than people. No matter the artistic liberties that were taken by Anglo-Saxon clerics, we can't deny that Vikings carried out violent and destructive attacks. But reducing the Vikings only to their warrior ventures is a grave mistake.

These Scandinavian men were indeed great fighters and military tacticians, but they were also merchants, explorers, artists, storytellers, and poets. They came from a rich and complex culture that they shared and left behind in the numerous lands they conquered or settled in. The Vikings' maritime voyages seem to have always been driven by two factors. One is the raiding and the plundering, and the other is the sheer sense of adventure and desire to discover new places. Around the eighth century, this led them to venture into the Faroes, which they used as a ***longphort*** (a fortified port) to advance across the Atlantic.

In 872, Viking colonists led by Ingolf Arnarson settled on Iceland, where they established a unique, independent society. This Icelandic settlement went on to become a republic, ruled by the Althing, an assembly of chieftains considered one of the earliest parliaments. From this Scandinavian settlement, we also have some of the earliest Viking-written history pieces, the ***Islendingabok*** - the history of Iceland and the ***Landnamabok*** - an account of the first Icelandic Viking settlers and the land lots they took as their own.

Besides these historical pieces, the Vikings who colonized Iceland also kept a written account of the tumultuous relationship they had with Iceland's natives. In the ***Islendingasogur*** (The Icelandic Family Sagas), the Vikings speak of the feuds, betrayals, allegiances, and conflicts that marked their first 150 years of settling in Iceland. The tales from the ***Islendingasogur*** are today considered to be some of the most important pieces of European literature from the Middle Ages, and they show the Vikings' proficiency in composing prose of great power.

Iceland also served as a platform for further exploration. In 982, Eirik the Red, a chieftain with a fiery temperament, was exiled from the Icelandic colony for his involvement in a murder case. Unphased by this development (perhaps due to his history of being an exile from Norway for another murder-related affair), Eirik decided to take to the sea, and he sailed west in search of a rumored land. A 300-kilometers voyage brought Eirik's longship to Greenland, a lush land that exceeded his wildest expectations. With this discovery on hand, Eirik the Red returned to Iceland, filled 25 longships with colonists, and established his settlement in Greenland, one that would survive well into the 15th century.

Eirik's son, Leif, a name you are probably familiar with by now, outdid his father as an explorer, sailing further west and discovering Vinland, but as a colonist, he wasn't as prolific as Eirik. Leif tried to replicate his father's strategy; however, the hostility from the Native Americans was too much for the small number of Viking settlers to handle, and Vinland was subsequently abandoned.

Regardless of his success at colonizing America, Leif Erikson has garnered the reputation of a great discoverer and explorer, and for a Viking, few things mattered more than their reputation. Sure, attributes such as bravery and intelligence were sought after in a Viking warrior, but leaving a legacy behind and being remembered was the icing on the cake. An aphorism from the *Havamal*, a collection of Viking sayings, goes something like "***Everything dies, we, our cattle, our families, but one thing that never dies is a dead man's reputation.***" The language used in the ***Havamal*** is a bit more sardonic, but I tried to give it a modern twist to better reflect the idea.

Daily Life of Norsemen

The Norsemen, as we call them today, were not connected to the name or function of Viking when at home in their Nordic countries. If you had to live there by that time, Norse or Viking would not be a word you understood or conceptualized the way we do in the modern world. You would be a part of a people who lived simply in the Scandinavian wilderness and who hunted, farmed, fished, cultivated livestock, spoke to the gods, and, at times, partook in a civil war among neighboring villages and clans. Positions of the hierarchy were established and overthrown many times, and slaves were commonplace. Kings and magnates (chieftains) were quite literally the men who owned the biggest farm or the most ships. Each clan or merchant town stood independent from the other, and later, with social evolution, regions and kingdoms were formed.

A simple subsistence level of farm work and living in rural farmsteads was a picture of normal Norse life. Villages usually consisted of between 15 and 60 people depending on their location for trade and agriculture.

Throughout the Viking Age, social structures began to evolve and encompass three main tiers:

- The elite, who were the wealthiest families like kings or chieftains.

- The free men and women. Here we see the majority of the population who might have owned their land, worked the farm, or traded goods and slaves.

- Slaves were known as thralls. Before slavery ended towards the late Middle Ages, the purchase and sale of human lives were considered standard practice.

Mortality rates were also very high and it is said that around 30–40% of children died before adulthood due to famine and diseases. We could see why the Vikings decided to venture to new lands, as theirs was hostile and unforgiving, especially in winter.

The trade routes of spices, silk, pottery, and silver were established and became a vital source of income as well as the trade of knowledge and information.

Many historians turn to the belief that Viking raids were assembled first and foremost to enslave the local people and take them back to their country to make use of or trade with. Mainly women were captured, but men and children were also taken. The slave trade focused on the continent of Britain but also extended across the Mediterranean from Spain to Egypt.

The evidence seen besides oral accounts is in the finding of collars and shackles around the ancient urban centers. Slaves were used for many activities such as textile manufacturing, shipbuilding, farming, and most of the unpleasant jobs done around the homestead. Sexual slavery and intermarriage were another reason the Vikings traded so loosely with the slave women and children of England and France.

Kings and chiefs played a central role In the ritualistic practice of public acts and meetings. A ***thing*** was a gathering of various clans and villages, and the law meetings in halls were presided over by the law speakers. Law speakers had to memorize the ***Bjarke*** law, which regarded smaller merchant towns. A group of Þing, who were free men and women from the villages, often voted and gave a say in these gatherings, whether criminal or political.

Later in the 11th century, especially in Iceland, the law became written text. Depending on the Nordic country, criminal proceedings were addressed slightly differently. Punishment most often included fines and, depending on the severity, outlawing, which meant you were no longer protected by the law and therefore capable of receiving any kind of punishment seen fit, something like village justice. Stealing, murdering, raping free women, and even lying and cheating were concerns brought forward to the earls and leaders of the regions for evaluation.

After the influence of Christianity, the proceedings altered and became more civilized. Slavery was abolished and many painful pagan trials to establish innocence were later abolished too.

The Creation Story

The ancient Nordics have a different version of creation. But like any other story of creation, in the beginning, there was nothingness. There was only this vast abyss within that infinite nothingness.

The first land formed was the world of elemental fire or Muspelheim, also called Muspell. This world was a place of light and heat. Its fire was so immense that no one could survive in it except those who dwelled there from the beginning.

This world had fiery rivers whose deadly waters formed into a solid mass. The guardian of Muspelheim was a fire giant called Surt. Surt is Old Norse for "black" which may refer to the giant's charred look.

He settles along the border armed with a flaming sword. Surt led the giants against both the Aesir and Vanir gods. He would be the slayer of Freyr, who was also the reason for the giant's demise during the Ragnarok.

Another world existed and this was the realm of elemental ice, Niflheim. This cold world was the complete opposite of Muspelheim. It was filled with wind, rain, and ice. A fountain called Hvergelmir stands at the heart of the Dark Land. From this fountain came glacial waters that formed the twelve rivers that flow through the void.

In the middle of the two worlds was the void known as the Ginnungagap, which means "abyss" or "yawning void." This ancient void was bounded by Muspelheim to the south and Niflheim to the north.

In this void, the heat from Muspell interacted with the coldness of Niflheim. The high volume of rain, glacial rivers, and masses of ice of Niflheim combined with the sparks, smoke, and glowing masses of Muspellheim, causing the ice to melt.

The drops from the melted ice created Ymir (Aurgelmir in some accounts). He was the first of the frost giants.

The androgynous Ymir could reproduce asexually. And he did so on the evening of his creation.

After falling asleep near the fiery Muspelheim, Ymir started to sweat. And from his sweat, more giants were born. His left arm created a son and a daughter while his legs bore him a son.

The frost melted further to create Audhumbla, a cow with life-giving milk. Ymir survived by suckling nourishing milk from Audhumbla. The cow, meanwhile, licked the ice blocks nearby to keep herself nourished.

After a day of licking, out came someone's hair from the salty ice. Audhumbla continued to lick the ice, and after two more days, a whole head could be seen. Another day later, Audhumbla released the whole of a strong beautiful man. He was the Norse god, Buri.

Buri was the first of the Aesir gods. He sired a son he named Bor who would later be wed to Bestla, the daughter of Bolthorn, also called Boelthor. Other texts say that Ymir himself was the father of Bestla.

She also had a brother who remained unnamed though scholars believe him to be Mimir who would later be beheaded by one of Bestla's sons. Bor and Bestla's union would be the first between giant and god. Their marriage bore them Odin, Vili, and Ve.

The three half-god and half-giant brothers would be instrumental in the creation of the world. The three conspired to murder Ymir and the rest of the giants. They started with their maternal grandfather.

After killing Ymir, blood flowed from his body. The volume of blood was so immense that the void was filled with it. The rest of the giants, save for Beregelmir and his wife, drowned in the blood of Ymir. The surviving giants escaped drowning by boarding a small boat. They would later start a new race of giants.

Odin and his brothers lifted the lifeless body of Ymir from the overflowing blood. They used it to create earth which they placed between Muspelheim and Niflheim. The giant's flesh became the land while his blood turned into the ocean.

The mountains were created from his bones while trees from his hair. They also turned Ymir's skull and four pillars of bones into the sky or Vault of Heavens. The gods assigned a dwarf to hold each corner of the sky.

The other gods appeared and learned of the brother's exploits. They proceeded to aid them in the creation of Asgard just above earth or Midgard. In "The Dwelling of the Aesir gods," each of them built their mansion or hall.

They also made the Bifrost, a rainbow bridge that the gods used to travel from Asgard to Midgard. The god Heimdall stood guard of the Bifrost. They also used the fallen giant's eyebrows to create a fence to protect them and the Midgardians from the giants.

The gods then saw maggots on the rotting corpse of the fallen giant. These grubs were transformed into dwarves. The creators decided the dwarves should stay hidden from the sun and within the earth or the flesh of Ymir.

Those dwarves touched by the rays of the sun were turned to stone. They bore no children as they were all male; so, the gods decided to make a couple of dwarf princes capable of creating other dwarves from the soil and stones.

The first human beings, or Midgardians, were fashioned from tree trunks. Odin, Hoenir, and Lodur were traversing the seashore when they saw two trees with warped trunks.

Odin molded the trees into the shape of a man and a woman and gave them life by breathing into them. Hoenir followed by providing the beings with souls. He also gave them the ability to reason. The other god, Lodur, presented them with warmth and the colors of life.

In another version, it was Ve and Vili who accompanied Odin during that walk. Vili provided the humans with the power of movement and the ability to understand while Ve gave them clothes to wear. He also gave the beings their names. Ask became the first man and Embla, the first woman. The two would go on to start the human race.

Norsemen is a term used for the Nordic people who lived in the North Atlantic region of what we know today as Scandinavia (Norway, Denmark, Sweden, and later, Iceland). An Old Norse language was established based on Germanic and Indo-European origins before the Viking Age. Although basic agriculture collapsed by 550 C.E. and was only restored towards the 8th century, historical evidence begins to show us a more detailed picture of set practices and beliefs coinciding with foreign influences. A more controlled paganism, if you will.

Their early society was not technically a literary one, and looking into their lives requires an understanding of their oral tradition, seen in early rune inscriptions and later in the sagas and poems. The stories were told, but the reasons and methods were left for interpretation.

The Norse were predominantly farmers, fishermen, and traders. It is often overlooked that their lifestyles were more than just pillaging and conquering. Their connection with their mythologies and their rituals of magic is rooted heavily in their actual day-to-day lives, rather than it being, for instance, a civilization polarized by different beliefs. They were unified and complex.

Norse Gods and Goddesses

The Norse gods are of three classifications:

• *The Aesir*

They are the gods of heaven, strength, and warrior might. Norse mythology holds that the Æsir lived peacefully in the fortress of Ásgarðr, built on the heights of the very high mountains of Ásaland, a land located in the center of the world. From this area, it is assumed they ruled the world, men, and elements.

• *The Vanir*

The gods of the earth, fertility, and magic. They settled in Vanaheimr, a remote area, but are in close contact with the natural cycles of the earth. From there, it appears that they dominated magic and had ties with humans and nature.

• *The Jötnar*

Residing in the realms of Jotunheim and Muspelheim, they are giants with superhuman strength, capable of creating chaos and devastation, and were in constant war with the Asgardians. They are evil, but gifted with great intelligence.

The two divine lineages (Aesir and Vanir) had always been hostile to each other. Because of this, two major wars for supremacy occurred.

The peace between the Aesir and the Vanir came with the stipulation of a sacred pact at the end of the second war, which established the superiority of the Aesir and a sort of integration between them.

Let's take a look at some of the big players in Norse mythology.

The Aesir

Odin

Odin is by far the most important god in Norse mythology. He was around almost from the beginning, helped create the cosmos, and ruled Asgard. He is known as a god of war, magic, wisdom, and even poetry. He was terrifying on the battlefield, making him a great warrior. At the same time, he only ever spoke in poems. These poems were so beautiful that others couldn't help but listen to him.

Odin only had one eye, and the story of how he lost his other eye is famous. One thing Odin wanted more than anything else was wisdom. Wisdom means knowing a lot, and Odin wanted to know everything. In Norse mythology, if you wanted wisdom, you had to go to the Well of Urd, also called Mimir's Well, because it was the home of a being called Mimir. The water of Mimir's Well held all the knowledge in the cosmos. Odin went there to ask for a drink so he could have more wisdom, too.

Mimir couldn't just give the water away since knowledge is very valuable. He asked Odin for an eye in return for a drink of water. You can probably guess what happened next. Since he desired wisdom, Odin gladly gave over an eye and then drank from the well. However, no one knows exactly what he learned when he drank the water.

An eye wasn't the only item Odin gave up in exchange for knowledge. Another story tells of him hanging himself from Yggdrasil for nine days and nights to learn about the runes, the same instrument the Norse people used as their alphabet. Remember that the runes are both letters and symbols of ideas. So, Odin wasn't just trying to learn the alphabet. He wanted to know what the runes looked like and meant because their symbols contained magic.

The wisdom Odin got from both the well and the runes made him one of the wisest and most powerful gods. His knowledge is one of the reasons why another name he went by was "Allfather." He had the power to give life or take it away, and he did both a lot of the time.

Baldur

Baldur is the son of Odin and Frigg. He is the god of light, sun, and joy. He makes everyone happy and shines with the light that comes from his skin.

The main story about Baldur is how he died. He started dreaming about his death, which scared his mother, Frigg. She asked everything that existed to promise not to hurt Baldur. She asked for weapons like spears and axes and even plants like trees and flowers. The one thing she didn't ask to hurt her son was mistletoe.

Loki, the mischievous god, convinced another god to throw mistletoe at Baldur because nothing else could hurt him. The mistletoe killed Baldur, and he went to the underworld, Hel. One of Baldur's brothers took Helvegr, the road to Hel, to try to get his brother back. He couldn't, so Baldur stayed in the underworld forever.

Thor

Everyone knows about the superhero Thor, but the Norse god Thor is a little bit different. He is the son of Odin and Jord, who was a giant. This makes Thor a giant too since his father is half-giant.

Thor is the god of thunder. He is the perfect example of an ideal warrior. Every Viking looked up to Thor. He is courageous, strong, and a loyal defender of Asgard.

While Thor also had a belt that gave him strength, his most famous possession is his hammer, Mjöllnir, which means "lightning." The lightning hammer used by the thunder god is one way how the Norse explained thunderstorms. When you hear thunder and see lightning, it's Thor riding on a chariot in the sky, slaying giants.

Since Thor is the god of thunder, he also has some power over rain. The Norse believed he could help their crops grow by controlling the weather.

Frigg

Frigg is considered the Queen of Asgard, which places her at the highest position of all the goddesses. Her name is sometimes spelled as Frigga. She lives in Fensalir, which means "hall of the marshlands," and is married to Odin. Her father was Fjorgynn. Considered the goddess of motherhood, she is the mother of Hermod, Balder, and Hodor.

She is also the goddess of marriage. The name Frigg comes from the verb "Frija," which translates to love. The word Friday comes from her, and so it is believed that Fridays are the best day to get married. Frigg also works a large blue cape, which symbolizes the sky.

While Frigg may have been married to the god of wisdom, she was very good at outsmarting him. They would often make bets on things. Odin would also come to Frigg for advice about certain issues, and while she didn't make predictions, she did know a lot about the future.

Despite her status as the goddess of marriage, Frigg was unfaithful to Odin on a number of different occasions. Some of her infidelity happened when Odin was exiled from Asgard for some time. During this time, his brothers Vili and Ve were placed in command. Besides presiding over the realm, the brothers were regularly sleeping with Frigg until Odin came back.

Being the Queen of the goddesses, Frigg was constantly surrounded by other women. Her attendant was Fulla, who had a gold band in her hair. She would look after Frigg's ash box and her shoes, and she also knew about all of Frigg's secrets. She had another attendant named Gna, who served as her messenger. If Frigg wanted to protect somebody, she would send out the goddess Hilin.

Despite her high position, the primary sources on her give only sparse and casual accounts of what she did. The specifics that are discussed about her are not unique to Frigg, but are shared with Freyja. With all of these similarities between the two goddesses, combined with their mutual evolution from the early Germanic goddess Frija, they only become nominally distinct figures during the late Viking Age.

In the poem "Lokasenna," Loki slanders Frigg, and then Freyja warns him that Frigg knows all beings' fate, which hints at her ability to perform seidr. Frigg has a set of falcon feathers that she uses to shapeshift into the bird.

Heimdall

Heimdall (HAME-doll) is the watchman of the gods. He is an Aesir god and a vigilant guardian. He was the whitest skinned of all the gods, and was often referred to as the shining god. Where he dwelt was known as Himinbjorg, or "Sky Cliffs," which is located at the top of Bifrost. It is believed that he could see 100 leagues, needed less sleep than a bird, and could hear the grass grow in the fields and wool grow on sheep.

He held the "ringing" horn, known as Gjallarhorn, which was loud enough to be heard all through the earth, heavens, and the lower world. It was this horn he would sound to summon the gods whenever their enemies, the giants, grew closer to them during Ragnarok. Once that time came to pass, Heimdall and Loki, his enemy, would slay one another.

Old Norse poetry seems to paint a picture that Heimdall was once thought to be the father of mankind and may have created the hierarchical structure of the Norse society. Like a number of other Norse deities, he is the son of Odin. In a feat only gods could achieve, he was born from nine mothers. Some people have tried to figure out who his nine mothers were, stating that they had to be the nine daughters of the sea giant Aegir, but this is a tough idea to get behind because the names of his mothers didn't match up with any of Aegir's daughters' names.

While Heimdall never had any wives or consorts, he did reproduce on occasion with the humans. It is believed that his anonymous children were the progenitors of the three classes of humans.

Much like Njord, the etymology of Heimdall is uncertain. It appears to be the combination of words that mean radiant, world, and eminent. That is why the literal translation of his name is given as radiant world. It could also mean "the one who illuminates the world." He was depicted as having golden teeth, so this makes sense.

A lot of the information out there about Heimdall only offers tantalizing scraps of information about this god. For example, he tends to be associated with the ram, but despite some speculative interpretations, this connection is still unclear.

Idunna

Idunna (EE-doon) is the goddess of youth. Her name means "rejuvenator" or "ever young." This goddess was born of flowers and lives in Asgard. She is in charge of growing the golden apples that help keep the gods young. She is married to Bargi, who is the god of poetry, and who is sometimes referred to as the "husband of Idunna."

Considering there isn't a lot of lore left about Norse mythology, we still know a fair amount about Idunna. One of the more popular stories about Idunna is the time when she was stolen away. The story starts out as such: Loki is stolen away by a great eagle, who turns out to be the Jotun Thiazi. Thiazi is very powerful and says he will only let Loki go if he agrees to bring him, Idunna and her apples.

Loki does as he asks, likely thinking he would find some way to bring her back. The kidnapping of Idunna and her apples throws the gods and goddesses of the Aesir and Vanir into an uproar because now they have started to age. Of course, they learn of Loki's role in this whole debacle. They force him to rescue her. He borrows Freyja's falcon cloak to transform into a falcon and flies to Thiazi's home, where he transforms Idunna into a walnut. Holing the walnut in his talons, he flies back as quickly as he can. Thiazi begins to chase after them but eventually gets killed.

This causes Thiazi's daughter, Skadhi, to show up at the gates of Asgard, demanding vengeance. She ends up accepting one of the Vanir in marriage as a form of repayment, and becomes an ally for the Aesir as well. So, it could be said that Idunna helped to create an alliance with Jotun. Ironically, Skadhi's gifts and realm are opposed to Idunna's.

Since Idunna is connected to both apples and nuts, she is considered a goddess of fertility. There are other hints that she may have had an otherworld nature. Apples and nuts have been associated with the otherworld and are often found on Germanic graves. In the poem "Hrafnagaldr Odins," it is said that Idunna was of the Elvin race. There is a lot of speculation about this mention of her in that poem. This reference is a bit confusing as it also refers to Idunna as Nanna, which could be why Aswyenn thinks they were sisters. The word "Alfen" in the stanza refers to Ivaldi, who is known as a Dwarf since the Duergar were sometimes referred to as Scartalfar or "dark elves." It could be that Idunna is the daughter of a dwarf and elf.

This same poem also suggests that Idunna may be responsible for nourishing the World Tree, Yggdrasil, through Ragnarok. It indicates that she conceals herself in the trunk of the tree. If pagans honored her, she would likely have been seen as a goddess of fertility due to her connection with apples.

Vidar

Vidar (VID-dar) is part of the younger generation of gods who make it through Ragnarok. However, that is true for only some accounts of Ragnarok. In other stories, the universe completely ends, and nobody survives. His name translates to "The Wide-Ruling One." Nearly every mention of him in Old Norse writings is about his role in Ragnarok. There is very little information available about his personality or function outside of one event.

During Ragnarok, the gods and giants battle, and the majority of those involved are slain. Odin is devoured by the world Fenrir. Vidar, who is the son of Odin and the giantess Gridor, sets out to avenge the death of his father. One of the shoes he wore had been crafted for this moment. It had been created as the sturdiest and strongest of all shoes and had likely been charged with magical abilities. With the shoe, Vidar kicked the wolf's lower jaw open, and then, as he held the upper jaw, he sliced Fenrir's mouth to pieces with his sword. This kills the world and brings an end to his rampage.

There is another mention of Vidar in which he is referred to as the "silent god," but there is no explanation as to why this name was given to him. He is believed to be the strongest of the gods, after Thor, of course. His home is filled with tall grass and brushwood, but the significance between him and this type of landscape is not known.

There are two places in Norway that include his name: Virsu "Temple of Vidar" and Viskjol "Pinnacle of Vidar." This suggests that he was likely a big part of pagan religious practices and was not seen as just a literary figure.

There are archaeological records that depict a man tearing apart a wolf's jaw on the Gosforth Cross in Northern England as well as the Kirk Andreas Cross in the Isle of Man. These are both dated around 900 CE, and they could be referencing Vidar and Fenrir. However, it is also possible they could be referencing Christ and the general world since Christ triumphing monsters was a popular motif used during medieval art. Even if these works of art were in reference to Vidar and Fenrir, it doesn't provide us with any new information, but just helps to corroborate what we already knew from literary sources.

This means that the only information that we really have about Vidar is that he avenged his father's death and killed Fenrir. The few other bits and pieces about him don't add up to much of anything, and they don't paint a picture of his personality or religious role.

Tyr

Tyr is the ultimate war god. He was very important to the Norse people, who valued strength in battle, law, and justice. Try represents all these elements. Vikings would often ask Tyr for strength in battle and to help them achieve victory.

Tyr didn't just symbolize war, though. He believed in fairness and justice. He was almost like the judge and jury of the Norse gods. There's one story with Tyr that shows just how much he cared about his fellow gods.

One of the most famous and terrifying creatures from Norse mythology is Fenrir the wolf. Fenrir was one of Loki's children. All the gods were afraid of Fenrir because of how strong and scary he was. They decided that it would be safer to lock him up, but he broke out of every chain they put him in. Finally, they had the dwarves make an unbreakable chain. Fenrir thought they were testing his strength, but the chain looked weak to him. Fenrir thought the gods might be tricking him, so he asked for one of the gods to put his hand in his (Fenrir's) mouth to prove that they weren't. Tyr was the only god who was brave enough to stick his hand in the wolf's mouth. When they wrapped Fenrir in the chain made by the dwarves, he was finally trapped. Fenrir was so mad that he bit Tyr's hand off.

Loki

Loki is famously known as the trickster god. While most of the other gods like and take care of each other, Loki is the outcast. He goes back and forth between helping the gods and helping the giants. He can be playful and funny, but he's not a nice guy most of the time. In many of the stories about Loki, his tricks get him into trouble. One of these stories is about the making of Thor's hammer.

Thor had a wife named Sif. She had beautiful, long golden hair. One day when Loki was bored, he decided to cut off Sif's hair. Thor was very mad and threatened to beat up Loki. To stop Thor from hurting him, Loki promised to have a new head of hair made for Sif. He went to Nidavellir, the home of the dwarves, to have the head of hair made. Dwarves were the best craftsmen, and they were able to make new hair for Sif. They also made a ship named Skidbladnir that could fold up to the size of a pocket and a mighty spear called Gungnir.

Loki could have gone back to Asgard with the ship, spear, and hair, but he wanted to play another trick. He dared two dwarf brothers, Brokkr and Sindri, to make three more items that were even better than Sif's hair, Skidbladnir, and Gungnir. He promised that if they did, they could have his head.

Brokkr and Sindri worked and worked, and while they did, Loki, disguised as a fly, tried to bite them to make them mess up. They were able to make three more amazing products even with Loki's mischief. These gifts included a boar (a pig with tusks) named Gullinbursti that gave off light and could run on land, in water, and the air. There was also a gold ring named Draupnir that could make more rings, and, best of all, the hammer, Mjöllnir. All these creations were perfect, except Mjöllnir, which had a handle that was too short. Thor was happy with it anyway, and the other gifts went to Odin (the ring and the spear) and Freyr (the ship and the boar).

There was still one problem, though. The three gifts Brokkr and Sindri made were better than the first three, so Loki owed them his head. When they went to cut it off, he reminded them that he promised his head and not his neck. So, since Loki had bitten them when he was a fly, Brokkr and Sindri sewed his mouth shut instead of taking his head.

The Vanir

Freyja

Freyja, also spelled as Freya, is one of the leading goddesses in Norse mythology. She is part of the Vanir tribe but became an honorary Aesir after the Aesir-Vanir war. Njord is her father, and her mother is unknown, but it might be Nerthus. Her brother is Freyr. In late Old Norse writings, her husband is said to be Odr, which is likely Odin. This is a big reason why people believe that Freyja and Frigg are the same goddesses. With her husband, she was the mother of Gersemi and Hnoss. Her most important possession was a golden necklace called Brisingamen, which she bargained for from four dwarves.

Freyja is known for her fondness of love, beauty, fertility, and fine material possessions. Due to these predilections, she is said to be a "party girl" of the Aesir. There is one poem in which Loki accuses Freyja of having slept with all the elves and gods, including her own brother. She definitely liked to look for thrills and pleasures, but she is much more than that. Freyja is a volva, a professional practitioner of seidr, an organized form of magic. She was the one who brought this magic to the gods and then to the humans. Given the fact that she's an expert in manipulating and controlling the desires, prosperity, and health of others, she is a being whose power and knowledge are almost unparalleled.

Freyja is the most agreeable and is gentler than other Norse deities. Where Thor is known to have accomplished his goals through aggression, and Loki and Odin liked to use trickery, Freyja would use gentler persuasions of sex, gifts, and beauty to get what she wanted. While she was helpful and unselfish most of the time, she did have a darker side. Much like the gods, she also had a taste for blood and was not afraid to fight in battle.

Freyja didn't typically wield weapons of war, but she did have a number of accouterments. One of those things was a cloak made out of falcon feathers that allowed her to take flight, as well as anybody else who wore it. If she wasn't wearing it, she would allow others to borrow the cloak. Freyja also rode on a glittering chariot pulled by two black cats. She had a familiar hog called Hildisvini.

Freyja is also the one who presides over the realm of Folkvang. In Folkvang was Freyja's home called Sessrumnir, or "seat room." This is an afterlife where Freyja gets to choose half of the warriors who are killed during the battle to dwell. Fridays are considered "Freyja's day."

Freyr

Freyr, sometimes written as Frey, is considered to be one of the most widely attested gods in Norse mythology. He is associated with virility, prosperity, peace, fertility, and sacral kingship, as well as a good harvest, fair weather, and sunshine. He is a part of the Vanir tribe of deities but is an honorary member of the Aesir.

He is one of the most well-respected gods, and in one poem, he is referred to as "the foremost of the gods" and "hated by none." It's not quite understood as to what the reason for this is, but others' prosperity and wellbeing depended on him being benevolent. This would most often manifest itself in ecological and sexual fertility, wealth, peace, and bountiful harvests. The role he had in abundance and health were often symbolized by his flygja, which was the boar Gullinborsti, and by his enormous, erect phallus.

It comes as no surprise that he was a frequent recipient of sacrifices on a number of occasions, like the blessing of a wedding or when celebrating a harvest. During their harvest festivals, they would often sacrifice Freyr's favorite animal, the boar.

We know that his father is Njord, but his mother is unknown yet is presumed to be Nerthus. Freyr took many lovers, from goddesses to giantesses, and even his sister Freyja.

Freyr resided in Alfheim, which was the home of the elves. This might mean that he was the ruler of the elves, but this is not stated explicitly in any sources. The relationship between the elves and the gods is pretty ambiguous, and it allows for a number of different connections between him and the elves.

A signature possession of Freyr is his ship, Skiobladnir, which sails at all times with a favorable wind and, when not being used, can be folded up and carried in a bag. The ship's name translates to "assembled from pieces of thin wood" and suggests that it served as an archetype of ships that were made for ritual purposes and weren't meant to be used at sea. We know that ships played a big role in the religious rites of the Germanic people, which is similar to the role ships played in the Bronze and Iron Ages, especially for the Scandinavians.

On land, Freyr would travel in a chariot pulled by boars. This also can be seen in historical rituals. In medieval Iceland, a priest or priestess of Freyr would travel through the county on a chariot that held a statue of Freyr. When the chariot would come to a town or village, the people would lay down every iron object and would enjoy some time of joyful festivities and peace.

During the end-times battle of Ragnarok, Freyr and the giant Surt are fated to kill one another.

Njord

Njord (NYORD) is a Vanir god of the hunt, fishing, seafaring, and wind, but has also been connected to wealth, peace, and fertility. Despite being a Vanir god, he lives in Asgard in Noatun, meaning "ship-enclosure," which is located right next to the sea. This was likely his favorite place to be, as he could listen to waves all the time and enjoy the wind that came off the sea.

Njord led his tribe of Vanir warriors against the Aesir in the war. During the aftermath of the war, he would find himself exchanged for Hoenir, an Aesir. They had both been held hostage by their enemies to prevent any more conflict. Eventually, Njord, along with his children, would be accepted and admired by the Aesir. It was this friendship that would lay the groundwork for lasting peace.

The tale that features Njord the most is "The Marriage of Njord and Skadi." Skadi is a giantess who came to the Aesir looking to avenge the death of her father. As part of the settlement with her, they agreed that she could take one of the gods as her husband. By mistake, she picked Njord, believing he was Baldor. She had only been allowed to make her pick by examining their feet. They had a very unpleasant and short marriage. They spent half of their time in Skadi's home in the snowy mountains, which Njord hated. The rest of their time was spent in Njord's home, which Skadi hated. Since they could not agree on where to live, the two parted ways.

Njord has two children, Freyr and Freyja, but their mother is not Skadi. Their mother is his unnamed sister. He had his children after his marriage to Skadi. At least, that's according to Snorri Sturluson's Poetic Edda. Throughout Scandinavia, Njord has been a very important deity, and a number of towns have been named after him. Unlike the vast majority of the other deities, Njord was fated to survive Ragnarok and to be reborn into the world.

Unfortunately, there isn't much more known about Njord. Despite this, there is evidence that shows he was a very widely-worshipped god for the Norse people. The etymology of his name is also unclear, but one theory suggests that it comes from the Proto Indo-European word ner-, which means "healthy, strong, and vigorous." In Old Norse, it was the masculine form of "Nerthus," the goddess of peace. This has led some people to believe that Nerthus evolved into Njord, while others think that Nerthus's traits were spread across several Vanir deities.

The Rebirth of Norse Religion

After the thought-out replacement of Norse paganism and the thorough removal of its every trace, there was nearly nothing left but what the people knew at heart and a few inscriptions. Keep in mind; the church made sure to destroy all statues and altars. Thus, the followers had no way to practice their religion. All that was left was the word of mouth that helped pass on the customs between generations and regions until, as mentioned before, it reached Snorri Sturluson, who resided in Iceland.

Reykjavík

Here, it should be mentioned that Iceland was one domain where Christianity was met with strong opposition from the parliament, which split in half, each supporting a religion. Then, almost resembling the Aesir-Vanir war, the two opposing yet equal parties came to the solution of converting to Christianity while allowing the private worship of pagan gods. Hence, the reason why Snorri could learn, collect, and write freely about Norse mythology, religion, and traditions.

It is from here that we can trace the origins of Asatru. Keep in mind that it is a reconstruction of the Old Norse religion. After the religion was almost wiped out, the Asatruar managed to pick up the pieces, link them together, connect with the spirits of their ancestors and the forces of nature around them. Eventually, they extracted the foundations and core beliefs and values of Norse paganism and put it into a modern pagan religion that connects ancient times to current times.

According to the Asatru Alliance, while Asatru beliefs are based on interpretations of literary texts, mainly Snorri's Eddas, they still heavily rely on two other factors. The first is the external universe, which is proof of the existence of higher forces. The second is the internal universe, each person's instincts, and faith. The Asatruar believe that this continuous spiritual guidance helps them in their search for a concrete truth, as opposed to historically inaccurate texts that carry many interpretations.

Asatru is a modern pagan religion founded early in the 20th century, but it was only later that it managed to get recognition from the Scandinavian governments. In 1972, the Icelandic religious organization, Ásatrúarfélagið (Asatru Fellowship), was created. A year after, it was given legal recognition as a religious institute. While the religion seems newly formed, it is deeply rooted in the Germanic religions that came before Christianity. A more accurate term to describe Asatru would be "a reconstruction." Asatru is based on one of the religions practiced in Scandinavia, the Netherlands, France, England, and the rest of Northern Europe in the period preceding the arrival of Christianity. In other words, it isn't technically a newly formed religion as much as it is a revival of old traditions.

In Ancient Norse, Asatru means "belief in the Aesir." The Aesir being the Norse Gods. Because the religion was practiced across such a large region in the past, it acquired many names. Vanatrú, Forn Sed, Vor Sir, Forn Sir, Odinism, Wodenism, Nordisk Sed, and more. In English, it is known as Norse or Germanic Heathenism. While it is also known as neo-paganism, this term is neither accurate nor preferred by the practitioners, known as the Asatruar.

The foundation of Asatru lies in several Norse myths documented in ancient scripts, mainly the Poetic and Prose Eddas. As for the rituals, traditions, and values, these were explained and described in sagas and some surviving texts. Keep in mind, the Asatruar don't necessarily believe in the myths being historically accurate, and neither do they believe in the literal execution of some outdated rituals, like blood sacrifices. However, they do believe in the values and the way of living that the rituals and myths represented. Yet, the matter is much more complicated than that.

From its origins as a folk religion, Norse paganism went through a long journey to reach the whole of Northern Europe. Not just that, but religion also faced the threat of growing empires. It went from a place of massive popularity to become a hidden faith due to prosecution. Eventually, Norse paganism reached a point where it was almost completely extinguished. How was the Asatru religion reconstructed until it assumed its current form today? We can only understand this phenomenon by looking back at the origins of the Old Norse religion, which planted the seed for Asatru.

Many people throughout the Scandinavian countries and the rest of the world are turning back to Asatru as the answer to everything. This ancient religion dates back to the times when Christianity or the Jewish faith hadn't even taken shape. Call them "Heathens" or "Asatruar," the followers of this faith believe in going back to the old ways of their ancestors.

Asatru is a modern term and not a traditionally used word, unlike what most people believe. The origin of the word "Asatru" lies in the Danish "Asetro," which roughly translates to heathenism. The meaning of Asatru can be understood by separating its component words Asa and Tru. After dissecting the word into two parts, we can understand that it means "belief in the gods."

It was first used in 1885 in an article, and then it was used again in 1945. Some sources also claim that the modern rendition of heathenism in the form of "Asatru" was first used in 1873 as a part of Edvard Grieg's opera called "Olav Trygvason." The exact origins of this word are debatable, and different scholars have different theories.

Several other terms like "Heidni" and "Forn Sidr" are also used for heathenism. These are old terms traditionally used in the Old Norse language. Some people also call it "Odinism" because of the primary emphasis on the god Odin, who's considered the king of gods. However, "Odinism" has taken on a more negative connotation in the recent past due to the popularity of this word among white supremacy groups. We'll be discussing this issue further in the last chapter, and we'll explore what the actual practitioners of Asatru feel about this issue.

The exact age of this religion is not very clear either, but it's widely accepted that Asatru, in its original form, is much older than Christianity, Buddhism, and many other religions. Some people claim that Asatru could be almost as old as Hinduism, if not older. Asatru has also shown some Paleolithic characteristics like shamanism and some Neolithic features like the concepts of "honor" and "shame."

Asatru was slowly replaced by Christianity as the primarily dominant region of Iceland. The settlers from Iceland were influenced by Christian beliefs as they traveled to Europe, and some of them brought home their new beliefs. This caused a divide between the people who followed Christianity and those who followed Asatru. To handle this divide and stop the nation from splitting, the parliament of the Viking commonwealth decided to make Christianity the only religion of Iceland. The followers of the old ways continued their practices in secret, but slowly, Christianity took over.

The last bastion of paganism fell when Lithuania officially converted to Christianity in 1386. This marked the end of paganism in Europe, but the Indo-European gods continued to survive in other regions. India, for example, was one of those places where the pagan gods were still thriving. The pagan gods had their Vedic counterparts who were greatly similar in detail. Thor became Indra, Odin became Rudra, and so on.

Even though Asatru was almost completely replaced, it resurfaced in the modern era and started to attract more people. We will be looking at the emergence of Asatru and how it's becoming one of the fastest-growing religions in Iceland today. We will also look into the different aspects of Asatru's history and the traditional beliefs that Asatru and its followers hold dear.

The Asatru movement can be traced as far back as the 1970s when a wave of revival swept across the entire religious landscape. Germanic paganism was gaining traction, and people began to realize the importance of their old faiths. Everything took a concrete shape when the Íslenska Ásatrúarfélagið was founded on the first day of Summer Solstice in 1972. Also known as the Icelandic Fellowship of the Aesir Faith, this organization was among the first to kick off the neopagan movement.

The "Asatru Free Assembly" also came to be established in the USA soon after, and they later became the "Asatru Folk Assembly." This marked the spread of the Asatru faith throughout the world rather than being limited to the European continent. The spread of this old faith was cemented by the efforts of various individuals throughout the world. The "Asatru Alliance" has been holding an annual gathering of all its followers known as "The Althing" for over 25 years and customs like these are what keep this faith spreading.

The Asatruars believe their modern version of this religion is identical to the practices of their ancestors. This neopaganism tries to emulate all the practices and beliefs of their ancestors, and followers believe Asatru blends all the positive attributes from both the older tradition and the newer culture, which comes together to create something that resounds with the believers.

Almost every Asatruar will give you a similar answer when you ask them where they gained their insight from — the Norse Eddas. Since most of the religion was purged by the Christians who labeled the pagans as barbarians, there isn't a lot of content other than the Eddas left. Another credible source of information for those who reconstructed the pagan religion is folktales, which have been preserved since time immemorial and have been passed on from one generation to the other.

Modern Norse Paganism (Ásatrú) was established just half a century ago, in the 1970s. It was recognized as a religion by the Icelandic state in 1973. The poet Sveinbjörn Beinteinsson along with eleven other Icelanders lobbied the Icelandic government about recognizing Ásatrú as a religion after establishing a formal congregation. It is unclear whether the group were practitioners of the Old Norse religion or just studying it, but they succeeded in their task either way. Those 12 people then held a meeting on the First Day of Summer, an important pagan holiday that denotes the end of winter and the beginning of summer.

Beinteinsson, along with his small congregation, was a key figure in getting modern Norse Paganism recognized by the Icelandic government. The association that formed in the process was Ásatrúarfélagið, "the fellowship of those who are true to the gods," although it is often just referred to as Ásatrú. It is currently Iceland's most common and most fast-growing non-Christian religion.

Since that successful moment, Modern Norse Pagan organizations began to sprout all around the Western world. In the United States, Robert Stine and Stephen McNallen formed the Viking Brotherhood, later renamed "Asatru Folk Alliance." The Department of Defense officially recognized Ásatrú/Heathenry in 2017. That resulted in giving full religious rights to Heathens in every service branch.

In Great Britain, the Committee for the Restoration of the Odinic Rite was founded by John Yeowell and others.

While these three were the first recognized Modern Norse Pagan organizations, the interest in the faith kept growing, with other associations and organizations emerging and introducing new approaches and ideas. There are currently around twenty thousand Norse Pagans worldwide. The Asatru concept will be further developed in chapter 8, where the rediscovery of the Norse religion from 1800 to the present day will be discussed.

Chapter 2: The Norse Religion is an Animistic Faith

When it comes to placing animism alongside other belief systems, some of the theoretical challenges encountered in anthropology and religious history originate not from the early relationship of animism with a speculative notion of religious development but from the broad array of animistic cultures. As a paradigm, it is broader than polytheism and monotheism, while its definition is more difficult to explain. The term encompasses beliefs mostly in or from the "small religions" but says nothing about their diversity. As a result, secondary categories like totemism, shamanism, and ancestor propitiation are frequently used.

In any case, these sects do not represent a people's entire faith. They are, nonetheless, institutions that are not limited to one culture: the Australian totemic cults have a "family resemblance" to the African totemic cults, albeit their variances and nuances are numerous. Shamanism, which relies on ecstasy, may be traced from Greenland to India, and ancestor worship is not limited to East Asia and Africa. The frequent occurrence of organizations of beliefs that fit a specific design indicates a radically small number of viable patterns, and the principles of animism appear to have established the constraint on this. Animism places a high value on supernatural beings that are separate entities tied to certain places and people or exist in specific species and are self-contained in their interactions.

Each human interaction with the extraordinary must be treated as a separate incident in such a paradigm. Even if ceremonialism prioritizes a long-term moral relationship with specific supernaturals, individuals are susceptible to imagining other powers they may turn to in a pinch. In times of difficulty, allegiance might shift: gods were sold to neighboring tribes in Western Africa, and a dream of trading European goods has prompted a slew of new fundamentalist cults in Melanesia. The virtue of openness favors changes or eclecticism over religious chauvinism almost every time.

Individuals in all animistic religions must communicate to supernatural beings, not about philosophy or moral difficulties, but about pressing practical matters such as healing illness, securing food, and avoiding danger. Typically, true supernatural adoration is hard to come by. Creator gods are frequently depicted in myths and not in cults. The recently deceased are most strongly conceived of in ancestral cults; the initial clan ancestor, after all his symbolic significance, is removed from both community and the godhead. If animistic forces wield authority anywhere, it is in a particularistic, perhaps egoistic manner, penalizing persons for a ritual's neglect or taboo-breaking rather than acts of ethical neglect and secular violation.

Animistic beliefs do not easily integrate with governmental systems and are unlikely to do so in the future. When questioned whether animism's relationship with fewer, simpler cultures proves it to be the inherent (original) religion, only one answer which we don't know (and may never know) is what panhuman or pre-written, historic religion would have been like. Recreating proto-human language is a difficult challenge. If spirituality is defined as a system of important interactions between people and supernatural beings, societies without religion haven't been discovered, and it is possible to assume that religion is typically a vital center of a society, where institutions' legitimacy is determined.

The idea of mysterious spirits animating all of ecology, whether they were demons, fairies, shades, or fates with whom people might interact meaningfully, might be a thing from the past; ideologies assign qualities of initiative or response to nature. People's receptivity to personal vision has been engaged by animistic beliefs all over the world, allowing them to deal with it based on recognized meaning.

Ancient Norse Mythology People, Monsters and Creatures Characters Icon Set

Fenrir

Fenrir, the wolf who bit off Tyr's hand, is one of the scariest beasts in Norse mythology. Even the gods were afraid of him. Fenrir is Loki's son, which might seem weird since he's an animal. Gods could do that, though. Most of Loki's children were animals, not people.

Even when Fenrir was a baby wolf, the Aesir gods knew he would be very powerful. Since he was Loki's son, they were afraid he would be in trouble, just like Loki. They raised Fenrir in Asgard so they could keep an eye on him. It's a good thing they did because he grew very fast. The gods realized that to control him, they would have to chain him up before he got too big. Tyr put his hand in Fenrir's mouth so the gods could chain him up, and Fenrir bit Tyr's hand off. They tied Fenrir's chain to a boulder, and the gods put a sword in his mouth so he couldn't bite anyone else. Fenrir was so mad that he howled and howled, and all that howling made him drool. The drool formed a river that the Norse called "Expectation."

Fenrir wasn't stuck to the boulder forever, though.

Norns

Not quite goddesses, not quite giants or dwarfs, not quite human – the Norns are identified primarily as female beings, whose primary function is to foresee and govern the destinies of all living things, from the Aesir on down.

The Norns are not limited to the trio of Urd, Verdandi, and Skuld; there are many others, who are said to appear around a child when it is newly born, and foretell what that child's destiny will be. Accordingly, some Norns are perceived to be benevolent, while others are malevolent.

The easiest way of understanding the primary Norns is to compare them to the Greek concept of the Fates: they spin the thread of a person's life and measure the length of his or her life. Urd's name corresponds to the past, Verdandi's to the present, and Skuld's to the future.

The primary Norns are depicted as women wrapped in all-concealing cloaks seated next to a holy well. Scattered around them are various lengths of thread and many other items associated with weaving, such as distaffs.

Skuld, in addition to her function as a Norn, is also often listed as one of the Valkyries.

Jormungand

Jormungand means "Great Beast," and that's exactly what he is. He's a serpent (a giant snake) that is so big; his entire body surrounds Midgard. Jormungand is another one of Loki's sons. Just like Fenrir, the gods don't like him. Out of all the gods, Thor hates Jormungand the most. They fought twice, and the last time was in Ragnarök.

In their first battle, Thor was fishing with a giant named Hymir. Jormungand lived in the ocean between Asgard and Midgard, and Thor wanted to catch him. He almost did, too. Thor caught Jormungand on his fishing line, and Thor was reeling him in. Hymir, the giant was afraid of Jormungand, so he cut the fishing line and let the serpent go. Thor was so mad, he threw Hymir overboard.

Elves

Having mentioned elves, it becomes easy to discuss this particular group of living beings.

There is some confusion about the "dark elves" since they seem to be described as living underground in the same way as dwarfs—or black elves—do.

Likewise, there is some difficulty in determining who or what the "light elves" really are since there is such a strong connection between them and the Aesir that some scholars have guessed that they might be the same. Others think that the light elves might be the Vanir, and there seems to be some support for that theory in the association between the god Freyr and the light elves. The main idea seems to be that these particular elves stood in opposition to the giants, as the Aesir did.

As with the dwarfs, elves appear in the stories and sagas of Norse mythology, but to a greater or lesser degree depending on the tales themselves. Sometimes, they are merely used to set the scene for the hero, giving him a sign that he will be traveling into unknown lands or even into different worlds entirely. At other times, the heroes are marked out as being special by having some degree of blood relationship to the elves, implying that their ancestors intermarried with these otherworldly beings.

Nidhogg

Nidhogg is another serpent, but he lives under Yggdrasil. He eats the roots of the world tree, which is very bad for the tree. The Norse believed he was a kind of giant who was trying to destroy the cosmos and everything in it. During Ragnarök, Nidhogg left his spot under Yggdrasil to help the giants.

Berserkers and Úlfheðnar

The Norse people thought that they could learn a lot from nature. They had shamans, which were people who believed they could connect to the spirit world or change their shape and become the spirit of an animal. Berserkers were shamans that became bear spirits on the battlefield. They wanted to be as strong and fierce as bears, so they wore bear skins and roared. There were also úlfheðnar (oolv-HETH-nahr), which are shamans who become wolf spirits instead of bear spirits. These shamans wore wolf pelts and howled at their enemies.

Berserkers and úlfheðnar were also called "Odin's men" because Odin gave them their powers and ability to change shape.

Dwarves

We usually think of dwarves as short, fat, bearded men. The Norse didn't think of them this way, though. The reason dwarves are called "black elves" is that they are like the elves, only they are pitch black because they live underground. Their home is in Nidavellir, which is full of mines and tunnels where they dig for metals and gems to craft with. Dwarves love making things, and they're very good at it. In a lot of Norse stories, dwarves are the ones who make objects for the gods, like Fenrir's unbreakable chain and Thor's hammer. They also made things like Odin's spear, Sif's hair, Freya's necklace, and a magic ring.

Dwarves were even around during the creation of the cosmos. When Odin and his brothers used Ymir's body to make the world, they asked four dwarves to help hold up the sky. These dwarves are Austri, Vestri, Nordri, and Sudri. Each dwarf holds a different part of the sky. Austri holds the east, Vestri the west, Nordri is in the north, and Sudri is the south.

Valkyrie and Valhalla

The name Valkyrie means "choosers of the fallen." Valkyries are Odin's helpers. They are female spirits who collect the spirits of warriors and take them to Valhalla. They don't take every warrior, though. Odin tells the Valkyries which warriors he wants in his home. These warriors will eventually help Odin during Ragnarök.

Valkyries don't just take warriors who have died to Valhalla. On the battlefield, they also get to decide who lives and who dies. They're a little bit like the Norns, but they only have control over the fate of warriors, not everyone else.

There are a few more creatures and beings that the Norse believed in, but we don't know a lot about most of them. A lot of the stories are gone, or just bits and pieces of them are left. If you want to know about every single creature in Norse mythology, many books have more stories related to them. You don't have to stop learning about Vikings when you get to the end of this book!

Dísir

While the dísir are also said to be female spirits that govern individuals and families' fates, the primary difference seems to be that they may have been derived from the collective spirits of the family's ancestors. They function as protective spirits, looking after the destinies of their descendants. Festivals were held to honor these spirits, at which sacrifices were made, and prayers were said to invoke their favorable regard.

Humans

According to material in the *Poetic Edda*, the first man was named "Ask," and the first woman was named Embla. Their names are derived from trees: "Ask" from the ash tree, and "Embla" from either the elm or a vine. The stories of their creation vary from account to account; some say that it was Odin, Hönir, and Lothur who gave them important gifts, while others say that the three gods involved were Odin and his brothers Vili and Vé.

The fate of mankind during the upheaval and battles of Ragnarök is likewise embodied in one man and one woman, who is foretold to survive the end of the universe by hiding either in a sheltered wood or within the trunk of a tree. The woman's name is said to be Líf, while the man's is Lífthrasir.

Natural Elements

A significant part of Norse cosmology is that the world exists in a literal and symbolic fashion. That symbolic fashion provides a means for us to make better sense of the world and how it operates. This, in turn, facilitates our ability to better operate from the perspective of being multifaceted individuals existing on three levels: the physical body, the mental/emotional body, and the spiritual body.

A fairly common way that many Pagans approach this symbolic view is through the classic five-elements model conceived in ancient Greece. This view allows things to be understood categorically and thematically as made up of five elements, in whole or in part. These elements are Earth, air, fire, water, and spirit. It is important to keep in mind that in this view, and especially where magick is concerned, none of us **is** an element, and our magick is not naturally aligned to one element over others, although we may feel more comfortable with the energy of one or two elements over others. We are each a **compilation** of the elements, made up of each of them in equal amounts.

<u>**Earth**</u>

Related to the physical Earth, this is the heaviest element and relates to things that are set, unchanging, and unmovable. It also relates to physical fertility, money and wealth, the home, animals, and plants. Earth teaches us the value of commitment, loyalty, and discipline.

It is typically associated with Winter and the colors green, black (think fertile soil), yellow, and brown. In the context of casting a circle (prominent within ceremonial magic, some witchcraft traditions, and some eclectic Pagan rituals), the Earth element relates to the northern quarter of the circle.

Air

Related to the sky, the air is an element of movement and change. It also relates to the mind and mental abilities and communication, divination, and travel. Air teaches you the importance of being open-minded, taking in information, and seeing things in new ways.

It is a hot and wet element associated with Spring and the color yellow and sometimes white, blue, or gold. In the context of a circle, it relates to the east and is where many magicians, witches, and pagans will begin casting the circle—as the sun and moon rise in the east.

Fire

Perhaps the most puzzling element, fire relates to the chemical process that we know as fire and the visible component of flame. The element of fire is transformative but also destructive, as anything that is transformed must have its old form destroyed for its new form to take shape. Fire relates to the sun and the spark of life and passion (in the sense of romantic attraction), love, anger, rage, bloodlust, and violence. Fire is also a protective element, as it can keep things at bay, and it can be used for healing in the sense of burning away disease and infection.

Fire is associated with Summer and is described as hot and dry. In the circle, it correlates to the south.

Water

Related to its namesake, the element of water is associated with movement, flexibility, dreams, emotions, the moon, and psychic abilities. Water teaches us to let go and move on.

Spirit

As nebulous as fire, the element of spirit is frequently misunderstood. It is that animating force within each of us, that bit of us that is enduring and eternal, that transcends personality and physical form.

There are no tools relating to the element of spirit, yet in the context of a ritual circle, the element of spirit is found in the center—where we place our altars and evoke the Gods, who are the ultimate embodiment of spirit.

The element of spirit reminds us that just as we are multifaceted and exist on multiple levels, so does the natural world. The spirit element keeps us focused on how much larger the world is than we can see, hear, and touch. It reminds us of the sacredness we each possess, the sacredness found throughout the natural world.

Chapter 3: Worship, Rituals, and Ceremonies

Ceremonies

Unlike the mainstream calendar, the ancient Norse calendar was split into seasons: winter and summer.

The start of summer ushers in with the festival of Ostara, which occurs close to the Spring equinox. In contrast, winter arrives with the festival of Winter nights, which is close to the Autumn (Fall) equinox.

In the middle of these festivals is Midsummer, also known as Lithasblot, which occurs on the summer solstice, and Jul (Yule) on the winter solstice.

Many of the festivals are celebrated with Blot rituals. For festivals and holidays, the Blot is largely focused on making sacrifices to the gods and spirits of the land. As mentioned previously, these sacrifices often take the form of wine or mead, or food.

While animal sacrifices were common in ancient times, it is quite rare in modern Asatru practices.

Of note is that the feasts and festivals mentioned below are the modern compilation of festivals that are believed to have held significance to ancient Norse heathens. Even in ancient times, different tribes chose to celebrate the festivals that they connected to the most. They might not have even held the same festivals as other tribes, or they might have held them at different times and in different ways.

Modern Asatru practitioners are offered the same freedom. What is important within this faith is doing what feels right for you.

Yule

Yule, or Yuletide. is a midwinter celebration that occurs on the winter solstice. Unlike the other festivals on this list, Yule doesn't have a set start date and has traditionally lasted around twelve days, with the sunset on the winter solstice marking the beginning of the festival.

The word Yule stems from the old Norse word Hjol, which means wheel. Therefore, it highlights the 'wheel of the year' when it is at its lowest point (*Yule*, n.d.).

This symbolizes not only the end of the year but a year ready to rise into a new year.

As with most of the festivals on this list, there are numerous accounts of how Yule was celebrated during ancient times, and these accounts vary from tribe to tribe. However, the consensus seems to state that it was a time of great celebration, giving gifts, dancing, feasting, and drinking.

Yule is an incredibly popular holiday and marks the return of Baldur from the realm of the dead and the end of winter. The first night of Yule is known as Mothernight, and during this time, Frigga and the Disir are honored. Mothernight represents the rebirth of the world. It represents not only the end of winter but also the birth of a new year.

In ancient times, a vigil would be held from dusk to dawn to ensure that the sun would rise. Ancient heathens would then welcome the coming sun. This time is also particularly sacred because it is the season when the deities are closest to our realm.

One of the customs of Yule is baking a boar-shaped bread which is then used to make the Yule-oaths, which are promises for the future. The western new year's resolution could stem from the tradition of the Yule-oath (*Yule*, n.d.).

Other traditions and customs include the Yule tree, which is a tree that is brought in and on which gifts are hung. The tree represents Yggdrasil, the world tree. During the 12 days of Yule, it is common for practitioners to do a lot of baking and decoration to make the home beautiful.

The 12 days of Yule are also believed to represent each month of the year, with the first day representing January and the second representing February, and so on. Therefore, it is often custom for practitioners to begin preparing for the coming year during this time.

Now, if all this sounds familiar, it is because the Christian holiday of Christmas takes most of its customs from heathen practice. The 12 days of Yule are also said to be the origins of the 12 days of Christmas, and the custom was probably adopted by early Christian missionaries. While the holidays share customs, the meanings behind them are completely different.

While Yule honors the gods Thor, Frey, Odin, as well as our ancestors, Christmas is celebrated in remembrance of the birth of Christ.

Disting (Disablot)

The festival of Disting generally occurs on the 2nd of February. This festival is also known as Oimelc.

The festival of Disting is the festival of the Idises. The Idises, also known as the Disir, are the spirits of the women in your family line. They are often the eldest mothers who are thought to watch over their children through the generations.

The Disting is also associated with the snow and cold and healing and the hearthfire. Ullr, Skadi, and Rind are the deities often honored during this festival (*Disting*, n.d.). These deities are all figures of the deep winter and are often associated with the cold.

Additional deities honored during this festival are the fire giants Logi, Glut, Einmyria, and Eisa, all of whom are associated with fire.

The festival of Disting is known as being the time where the land is prepared for planting. In ancient times, this would be the time that cattle and livestock were counted and wealth was tallied. Therefore, Disting can also be considered a festival of finance.

Calves born during this time were also considered a sign of prosperity for the year to come.

What makes the festival of the Disting so interesting is that it highlights the coming of spring. Therefore, it becomes a festival that balances the light of spring and the darkness of winter. While the coming of spring was celebrated, the ancient heathens were careful to honor the gods of winter and not offend them.

The Disting is a time for new beginnings and honors not only the past, shown by the honoring of the ancestors and the gods of winter, but also the future by honoring the gods of spring.

Ostara

The Ostara means the Spring Equinox and is celebrated on March 21 every year. Marking the start of the summer months, it is named after the goddess Ostara, an important Germanic deity who embodied spring and the renewal and revival of life. The name Ostara signifies the east and glory.

The Ostara festival is a celebration of the revival of the Earth after months of freezing cold winters. Traditionally, homes are decorated with flowered, colored eggs, budding boughs, and branches, *etc.* The hare was the spirit animal or holy beast of the goddess Ostara. Slaying and eating rabbit meat was allowed only after taking permission from the goddess.

Holding and keeping the Ostara feast enhances the joy and happiness of the festival participants.

Some common folklore traditions that have carried on from ancient times and continue even today include:

- Fires kindled at the top of hills at the break of dawn.

- The performance of plays in villages and rural areas. In these plays, summer and winter are shown as people battling each other, with summer winning over winter and driving him off the stage.

- Effigies representing winter are drowned, beaten, and burned to signify the end of winter.

<u>Walpurgis</u>

The festival of Walpurgis takes place between the 22nd of April and the 30th of April in remembrance of the Allfathers sacrifice upon Yggdrasil, the world tree. The nine nights between the 22nd and the 30th are venerated in honor of this sacrifice.

As the myth goes, Odin hung on Yggdrasil for nine days, gaining the wisdom of the runes. However, they came with a price. On the ninth day, Odin grasped the runes, and for a split second; he died. At that moment, the light of all nine worlds was extinguished, and chaos reigned. Then, at the stroke of midnight, Odin lived once more and light returned.

The 30th of April is known as Walpurgisnacht and is considered by some to be the most important part of this celebration.

Therefore, the commemoration of Walpurgis is a festival of revelry and darkness. It represents the moment when all could've been lost were it not for the Allfather, Odin. Unsurprisingly, it is also a festival that honors Odin.

Each group and individual celebrate Walpurgis in a way that feels right for them, and these practices differ. However, a common practice is that of the Blot.

Walpurgis can also go by the name of May Day, and with this name change comes a change in meaning.

May Day is celebrated in honor of Frey and Freya, the goddess of love. This festival is commonly associated with the celebration of love and may also honor minor love deities Lofn and Sjofn. If practitioners intend to make oaths on May Day, they might decide to honor Var as well.

Midsummer

The festival of Midsummer is by far my favorite festival. It occurs on the summer solstice, which is the 21st of June in the northern hemisphere. The date is subject to change depending on the season and the part of the world that you find yourself in.

Like most other festivals, rituals, and practices within the Asatru faith, the festival of Midsummer has numerous interpretations and meanings.

The most common interpretation of Midsummer, being the longest day of the year, is that it is a time of celebration, prosperity, trade, and if you're a Viking, a time for raiding. However, Midsummer has a darker side to it.

Being the longest day of the year, it goes without saying that the days following will be shorter and shorter as winter approaches. Therefore, while it was a time of celebration, it was also a time of self-reflection and contemplation as ancient Norse heathens prepared for the darker, colder times to come.

One of the myths closely associated with Midsummer is that of Baldur, the god of light. During this time, it is believed that Baldur is slain and, as winter comes, the Aesir goes into mourning for him. However, as winter comes and then retreats once again with the dawn of spring, the Aesir mourn and recover and thus can move on with their lives.

During the festival of Midsummer, some practitioners might also decide to send their blessings to Sunna, the sun, and honor her for her warmth and her life-giving light. It is also a time where Dagr, the god of the day, might be honored.

This period of the year is considered to be a time to still contemplate and recharge your physical and spiritual batteries in preparation for the coming spring.

Midsummer is thus a time for Blot rituals, sacrifices in honor of the gods, and worship. Typical traditions practiced during Midsummer are making wreaths, burning fires, little dolls made of corn, and adorning fields and houses with greenery. To honor the god Baldur, little ships might be made and filled with little offerings to the gods. These are burned in sacrifice to Baldur.

Freyfest or Lammas or Lithasblot

Lammas is believed to be an Anglicized word for "half-mass" or "loaves festival," a Heathen occasion of thanksgiving for bread. Heathens celebrate this festival by baking bread in the shape and figure of Freyr, followed by its symbolic sacrifice and consumption. The first of August is the time when the first fruits of harvest arrive, and in Germanic traditions, the first sheaf is offered to the Heathen gods in thanksgiving.

In today's Heathenism, Lammas (otherwise known as Lithasblot or Freyfest) is dedicated to Freyr, the fertility god, and Sif (Thor's wife), whose long golden hair is believed to symbolize the yellow fields of ripe and ready-to-harvest crops. The warriors who went to battle after the planting season returned home at this time with their battle winnings. Freyfest is the day when the hard work of harvesting and preparing for the cold winters begins.

Fall Feast

The autumn equinox – September 21 – may or may not have been celebrated; the Saxons referred to September as *Halegmonath* or Holy Month, so obviously something was going on, and there are references in Scandinavia to *Haustblót* or the autumn sacrifice. However, historically, everyone may have been too busy getting the harvest in to do more than have a ritual feast. Still, ritual feasts are sacred as well, and we just refer to this holiday as Harvest. Here we honor the Gods of food harvest – Frey, Nerthus, Iduna, Njord, and of course Jord. We honor Snotra as a goddess of hard work and hospitality, and Huldra as keeper of flocks. Bragi is honored again at this time for his storytelling, as is Saga the keeper of history.

Harvestfest or Winter Nights

This day marks the end of the harvest season. On this day, people would butcher the animals that are not expected to survive the harsh winters, and their meat would be made into sausages or smoked for use in the cold months. Also referred to as Frey-Blessing, Dis-Blessing, and Elf-Blessing, this festival is the time for honoring land spirits, ancestral spirits, and the Vanir gods.

It marks the beginning of winter. It is a time when everyone is expected to turn his or her perspectives from outward to inward. According to Norse traditions, the festivities of Winter Nights were officiated by the woman of the house, and the last sheaf was left in the fields for the gods, spirits, and deities.

The Winter Nights feast was celebrated by telling old tales of bravery and accomplishments and focusing on future achievements. The Harvestfest celebrated the power, veneration, and importance of our dead ancestors. Moreover, it reminded people of the important tenet of Germanic belief that death was not scary or evil. For the Nordic people, death was not as important a topic to ponder over as much as living and dying with honor.

May Eve

May Eve is a holiday celebrated on April 30. This festival is known after a woman called VA LBORG. She was born in 710 A.D. Valborg was the niece of the infamous St. Boniface.

The Celts called May Day – May 1 – Beltane, but in Germany, it was Walpurgis, again named after an obscure goddess, this time Walburga. Walpurgisnacht – April 30, the night before – is celebrated as the time Odin had hung on the World Tree for nine days and gained the wisdom of the Runes. May Day itself is associated with Frey – the great Maypole his phallus – and Freya as Goddess of Love. This is a day of merrymaking and the celebration of love, and Lofn and Sjofn, both minor love goddesses, may be honored. Var may be honored if people intend to take oaths on the Maypole. The Alfar, or Elves, are associated with this day, as is Mani, the Moon God who sees what people do in the bushes after dark, and Jormundgand, the great serpent of the ocean.

The Norse Rituals

The word ritual can sound very intimidating and seem as though they are these massive, daunting tasks. While this might be true in other faiths and religions, it is not the case within Asatru.

As with all heathenistic and pagan faiths, Asatru focuses on building and strengthening the relationships between practitioners and their surrounding community. This respect and focus extend to the spirits of the land you live on, to your ancestors, and the gods.

In many ways, rituals are vital for maintaining your relationship with the gods, your relationships with your community, and your relationship with your ancestors. It is the main way in which we honor the gods and thank them for their numerous blessings and favors.

Performing these sacred rituals is one of the main ways of worship within Asatru.

However, within the modern Asatru faith, the meaning of rituals has expanded and now represents not only our relationship with the gods but also a reclaiming of a faith that was almost lost during the conquests of Christianity.

After almost disappearing, Asatru represents a revival of the old faith and a reawakening of the gods after generations of being asleep. It is believed that if people stop believing in and speaking to the gods, they will fade away and die. By performing rituals and communing with the gods, you are keeping them alive; you are keeping them strong.

The relationship between the gods and practitioners is symbiotic. They need us as much as we need them.

While interpretations and practices of these rituals vary from practitioner to practitioner and from group to group, a few markers define Asatru rituals. During ancient times, Norse heathens would erect altars or set up hallowed locations that could be used for ceremonies of worship, usually by a group of Kindred.

The Godhi and Gydhja

Unlike the Abrahamic faiths, Asatru doesn't have a strict hierarchy of holy men and women. Within Asatru, there is only the *godhi* (God-man or priest) and the *gydhja* (God-woman or priestess).

However, the godhi and gydhja aren't necessary to practice Asatru because heathenry is not an organized faith.

The main purpose of a godhi or gydhja is to bring believers and practitioners together and help them grow their faith and strengthen their relationship with the gods. The purpose is to offer guidance and bring knowledge to the community.

Unlike with Abrahamic faiths, a godhi or gydhja aren't held up on pedestals. They are ordinary people like you and me, but with a different calling.

A godhi or gydhja may lead groups of kindreds or fellowships through rituals and celebrations, but a large majority of Asatru followers practice their faith as individuals.

Runecraft

One of the rituals that highly characterize the Norse religion is runecraft. Pagans would inscribe their prayers and songs for the gods in runes. Sometimes these runes are read, colored, and interpreted, and even used to predict the future. The major theme in Norse rituals is divided into three words: bithja (ask), blota (sacrifice), and senda (send). These words already give modern scholars of Norse mythology an image of how the ancient Norse people prayed and asked for blessings. There is an invocation involved – a call or supplication to the god. There is an offering to be made, which could be food, animal, or in some clans, the blood of humans. Then there is a sending of the message to the gods. In some cultures, the smoke that rises from the fire and reaches the heavens is a way to send the prayer and the sacrifice to the gods. If the gods are connected to the earth, such as the god of the harvest, the blood is sprinkled into the earth for the god's "consumption."

Seidh

The Norse practiced several rites, especially those of a magical nature. The term seidh originated from the ritual of the Norse to boil salt, which also happens to be a purification rite. Though women practice prophecy, men are equally capable. The Norse male practitioner is called the vitki. Being skilled in seidh is considered important in the Norse community, as seidh is Odin's specialty as well. With seidh, Norse sorcerers could shapeshift (or so they claim), send nightmares to people, conjure love spells, make women fertile, and raise storms.

Rites of Passage

Concerning birth, death, and marriage, these were also common rituals performed both in public and in private. The birth was viewed as dangerous for both mother and child, and galdr singing was often conducted in a ceremony to guide safe passage for the baby at the moment of birth. Prayers were sent to the goddesses Freyja and Frigg. Nine nights after birth, there was also a ritual not dissimilar to a Christian christening ceremony, in which guests were invited to bring gifts and give good wishes to the child. Water was sprinkled onto the baby while being held on their father's knee. In this way, the child was formally admitted into the family. Children were also named at this time, often after ancestors or deities, or both. Setting the child on their father's knee during this ceremony officially accepted that child into society and made the parents responsible for the child's wellbeing.

Beyond selecting one's mate and receiving family approval for that choice, which was often made by other family members in the first place, other rules and rituals were followed to summon deities to bless the wedding and avoid bad marriages. Naturally, there was no guarantee that these rituals would always prevent a bad marriage or separation. Betrothal dates were carefully set and inheritance, property, and dowry were negotiated. Once this was done, the gods were called in.

The most important ritual was the wedding itself (brudlaup). This was a public gathering of the two families involved and included a feast that lasted a minimum of three days. The goddess Var witnessed the vows. A depiction of Thor's hammer was placed on the bride's knees, asking Thor to bless her, and Freyja was always called upon to bless the marriage with fertility and luck as well. Guests would lead the bride and groom to bed. A group of witnesses would mark the consummation of the wedding and the marital relations between spouses to be legal.

The Rite of Birth

The conception and birth of a child are incredibly significant in Asatru. It is believed that once a child is conceived, the spirit of the future child is created. However, the spirit doesn't immediately enter the body of the child. Instead, it enters slowly, bit by bit, as the child grows and develops reason and intelligence.

Another belief is that, before the spirit can submit to being incarnated, the father and mother both need to understand that the child's spirit has existed before it is born into Midgard.

The actual birth of a child is very sacred. It is a moment that bridges the physical and spiritual worlds. Given the significance of this occasion, it is celebrated with the rite of birth.

The rite of birth is the first initiation, and it is aimed at the growth of the child's spirit self.

The godhi or gydhja performs a hammer hollowing, and once done, he recites the customary words and places oil on the baby's forehead. Lastly, he does the sign of the hammer, speaks the final words, and then the ritual is complete.

The words spoken and the signs shown can differ from practitioner to practitioner and from group to group.

Coming of Age Rites

The coming-of-age rite, called the Sidfesta, is generally held to mark the beginning of puberty, around the age of 13. However, when the practice rites take place depends on the child, their parents, and the practices they follow.

Not all Asatru practitioners mark the coming of age of a child with the traditional rites. In ancient and current times, children often follow the faiths and religions of their families, but Asatru is a bit different. In Asatru, the child needs to choose whether they want to be Asatru or not.

It is completely their choice.

Therefore, if the child decides to follow a different path, a coming-of-age rite is not necessary.

That being said, the Sidfesta is essentially a confirmation. It is a ritual that confirms a child's entry into the Asatru faith. Thus, it serves a similar function to a Christian confirmation ceremony.

The Sidfesta is also characterized by educating the child in the lore of Asatru, and discussions of ethics. There are also discussions surrounding what it means to be Asatru and the lifestyle shift that occurs once you make this decision. And, trust me, it is not a decision made lightly.

The process of Sidfesta is highly personalized and can be performed in numerous ways to suit the family's needs, wants, and beliefs.

Strangely enough, Sidfesta is not an ancient custom. Instead, it was born out of a modern need for present-day heathens. In many ways, the Sidfesta is also used as a means of entering the faith, although this rite is certainly not necessary to join the Asatru faith.

The Sidfesta is celebrated in numerous ways but is characterized by imparting knowledge onto the child and allowing them to interpret this knowledge as they wish. Other customs include allowing the child to go out into nature and find objects that they feel represent who they are. The child is then asked to explain each object and state why they chose it.

This practice is said to show that the child has reached a certain degree of maturity.

Often, the Sidfesta is celebrated with a Sumbel ritual, and, if the family wishes, a godhr might be present.

The Rite of Marriage

There are numerous forms of the rite of marriage. In this section, I'll be focusing on the hand-fasting rite of marriage.

A definition of the word 'hand-fasting' means betrothed or marrying by the joining of hands. In ancient times, the hands of the couple were tied together with a red cord by either a godhi or gydhja during the wedding ceremony (*Rite of Marriage Hand Fasting*, n.d.).

This is symbolic of their union and commitment.

Unlike western wedding customs, the clothing that the bride and groom wear is not prescribed. There are a few customs, but they are hardly set in stone. The color white is customary; however, the bride often wears white flowers in her hair instead of a veil.

In some practices, a sprig of rosemary is placed on the bride's bed as a token of good luck. Mandrake root is also placed under the bed as a token of virility.

Similar to western movies, the celebration starts with music, and the godhi leads the wedding procession carrying the sacred hammer of Thor. They are closely followed by the wedding couple and the groomsmen and bridesmaids.

In Asatru wedding celebrations, the groomsmen and bridesmaids act as torchbearers.

The procession will then approach a circle and the torches are carefully placed at the entry of the circle and they stop. The godhi alone enters the circle, and the bride and groom, armed with garlands and a horn of mead, set those down on an altar.

They then stand facing the horg, and the ritual officially begins. The godhi will often open the circle with a traditional speech of blessing and then walk sunwise around the circle before returning to the altar. They will then pick up a runestaff and approach the couple.

The godhi will rap on the ground three times before returning to the altar. Now, the rites of marriage vary from group to group, but generally, the godhi will anoint the couple with salted water and speak a blessing of Frigga.

Rings, called the hand-fasting jewelry, are then exchanged, and after a final prayer, the ceremony is over. The happy couple is required to keep their arms bound with the red cord until they leave the circle.

It is also common for couples to keep the cord as a reminder of their commitment.

The Rite of Death

Many cultures and religions believe in some kind of afterlife where the spirit goes after the body has passed on. The common theory is that there's heaven, the place you go if you've lived a good life, and then alternatively, hell, where you end up if you've lived a bad life.

Theories of what happens after we die vary from person to person and from faith to faith, but to be honest, no one knows what happens after we're gone.

According to the Asatru faith, we could end up in two places after we pass. The first, and probably the most desirable, is Valhalla, a grand hall where the departed dine with the gods. Unfortunately,

Valhalla and the honor of meeting the gods are reserved for those noble warriors who died gloriously in battle.

Those who died of sickness, old age, natural causes, or accidents are set for Hel. Now, this is not the Hel you're imagining. It is simply another version of the afterlife where we can rest in peace with family and loved ones.

Now, contrary to what you might've seen in the movies, the funeral rites don't involve flaming longboats.

In ancient times, honorable people were buried deep inside a ship filled with the things they might need in the afterlife. These ships were placed inside burial mounds.

An alternative practice was that of funeral pyres. It was believed that the huge pillars of smoke would aid the spirit in rising toward the afterlife.

It would be quite hard to erect funeral pyres or bury our deceased in the bellies of ships nowadays, so a few changes needed to be made.

The modern funeral rites involve burying the dead in a replica of Thor's hammer or placing it on the lid of the casket. If the deceased has been cremated, the hammer of Thor is burned.

<u>**The Blot**</u>

In ancient times, the Norse heathens were mostly farmers, and sacrificing animals was considered a great honor since the animal represented more than just meat; it was their livelihood. It embodied the strong bonds between the heathen and their gods. Understanding the relationship between the practitioner and the gods is vital when trying to understand the purpose of sacrifice.

It is believed that humans are intricately related to the gods, not only spiritually, but also by blood. In many ways, we are kin and form part of their tribe. Therefore, the sacrifice we make during the Blot, whether food or drink or animal, is us sharing what we love with the gods.

Giving gifts and sharing were important aspects of ancient Norse life and had incredible significance.

<u>**Sumbel**</u>

One of the most common celebrations noted in tales of our ancestors is the Sumbel or ritual drinking celebration. This was a more mundane and social sort of ritual than the blot, but of no less importance. When Beowulf came to Hrothgar, the first thing they did was to drink at a ritual sumbel. This was a way of establishing Beowulf's identity and what his intent was, and doing so in a sacred and traditional manner.

The sumbel is quite simple. The guests are seated, (traditionally, in some formal fashion), and the host begins the sumbel with a short statement of greeting and intent, and by offering the first toast. The horn is then passed around the table and each person makes their toasts in turn. At the sumbel toasts are drunk to the Gods and a person's ancestors or personal heroes. Rather than a toast, a person might also offer a brag or some story, song, or poem that has significance. The important point is that at the end of the toast, story, or whatever, the person offering it drinks from the horn, and in doing so, "drinks in" what he spoke.

The sumbel is also an important time for the folk to get to know each other in a more intimate way than most people are willing to share. People within our modern society often behave at one of two extremes. At one end are individuals who remain unnaturally distant from their own emotions, either because to display emotion would be "unmanly" or because they have been socialized to believe that self-sacrifice for others is the only desirable way to live. On the other side are those who cultivate their "feelings" and who spend their lives consciously attempting to stir their emotions and who force an unnatural level of intimacy between themselves and others. However, some levels of emotional intimacy are not meant to be openly shared with strangers. Doing so reduces their meaning to the mundane. At sumbel, barriers can be lowered in a place that is sacred to the Gods. Thoughts can be shared among companions and friends without embarrassment or forced intimacy.

The Profession

The Profession is an important ritual within Asatru. As the name suggests, the aim here is to profess one's belief in the gods and is considered a turning point in one's life and a step toward a deeper understanding of the self.

Unlike the Blot and Sumbel, the Profession is often quite short and can take place before and after another ritual.

The Profession is often performed by newcomers who wish to join Asatru and involves a godhi. The purpose of the godhi is to accept the oath; however, a newcomer does not need a godhi to join the Asatru.

At its essence, the Profession entails committing Asatru and the gods. It can also be interpreted as making an oath to honor the practices and beliefs of Asatru as well as the gods. As I've mentioned before, oaths should never be made in vain. Therefore, before performing the profession, you should think about the commitment you're about to make.

Another important point is that no one can be forced to Profess. False or coerced Professions cheapen the ritual.

Evocation and Invocation – Talking to the Gods

The first thing you must do when you get a calling to follow Norse Paganism is to just listen and talk to your gods. Remember that in Heathenism, gods are your friends and kinsfolk, and having conversations with them can build your rapport and help you understand what you need to do and how to move ahead.

Talking to your gods is a habit you must foster early on in your journey. Modern life is so rife with professional and social activities that we forget to have conversations with our gods. However, if you persist in building this habit, like other habits such as eating healthy, exercising, etc., it can and will become part of your life routine.

You can find gods all around you in the form of spirits. You can strike up a conversation with any of them whenever you want. There is nothing to be afraid of. You can simply go out there and start speaking to Odin, Thor, or any of the gods you believe in. A vital element when speaking to gods is to remember to do so with respect. Initially, you will not know how and what each god expects from you during a conversation. Respect is a safe place to begin your conversation.

For example, if you need to speak to Odin, the king of the pantheon of Norse deities, then it makes sense to see him as a leader or father figure who can give you the powers of wisdom and clarity of thought. When you summon him, do it with humility and respect and seek his guidance and wisdom.

With another god, for example, Loki, you could have a different approach. While respect is a given in every conversation with gods like Loki, you can easily take an informal approach and treat him like a friend or ally. Loki is a God who will give you what you seek but will also want something in return. So, there is a sense of give-and-take camaraderie with this god.

Another critical element about having conversations with Norse gods is to have a purpose. What do you want to ask your god? Is there something bothering you? Do you seek enlightenment, clarity, or a problem to be sorted? Casual conversations like how your day at work went should be avoided because it would be wasting the time of the gods. Remember to value the time they give you when they come to talk with you. It is important to make your time with the gods meaningful.

The second step in your Asatru journey is to collect knowledge and wisdom. Do a lot of research and learn about the Asatru faith. What does it mean? What is its history? Who are gods and goddesses? Why are they the way they are? What sets them apart from human beings? What are the roles of the various gods in Asatru?

Learn about Asatru's ancestors. As you learn more about the Viking and Germanic ancestors, you will find yourself unlearning many of the elements that got incorporated into the history of the Nordic people, wittingly or unwittingly. Remind yourself that the ancestors of the Germanic tribes were highly advanced and intelligent, built fast-moving boats, and were brave warriors. They traveled long distances, conquered many lands, and imbibed the culture and traditions of the conquered lands. Our ancestors could not have done so much if they had simply been savages or fools.

The more you learn about Nordic ancestors and ancient tribes, the deeper your faith will become. A great way to enhance the depth of your knowledge in the domain of Norse Paganism is to try to rephrase the books, poems, and prose you are reading and studying. Also, you could check out if translating your lessons into another language will help you. Not only will this exercise build your skills in another language, but it will also help you get a deeper understanding of Norse wisdom, mythology, and ancient, forgotten knowledge.

The third step to becoming a practicing Heathen is to give offerings to the gods. The offerings you give in the form of mead, wine, meats, cheese, and other foods empower the gods, and in an empowered state, they are in a better position to help you when you need them. Again, it is time to reiterate the importance of gift exchanges in Norse Paganism.

When you give a gift or offering to the gods, they return your favor multiple times because they feel empowered by your gifts. Knowing what gifts to give to which god should be part of your research and learning process. For example, Odin is a God who only drinks and does not eat anything. If you offer him meat or cheese or something else to eat, he will not be happy, and the chances of him helping you in return are slim. Mead would be the ideal offering to Odin. You can get such important information only when you keep reading, learning, and researching the Asatru faith.

The trick is to start small. Begin offerings in little bowls, create your hallowed verses, and seek the blessings of your gods. Don't forget to talk to them and ask them if they liked your offerings. The more you talk to them, the more you will realize that your gods are continually trying to send you messages and signs in different ways and through different people.

As you gain confidence in your ability to make offerings correctly, you can slowly and steadily enhance your offerings. Some people started with a small bottle of mead and have ended up building firepits into which they throw steaks and meats as offerings to their gods through the fire element, but don't hesitate to take those baby steps. Start now, and sooner rather than later, you will find yourself expanding in your Asatru journey.

The fourth step in your journey is to connect with more Pagans and identify yourself with a community you are comfortable with. Although Asatru is a sort of personal religion, it is also about ancestor worship, praying, dancing, and chanting together. It is about drinking consecrated mead together, and it is about worshipping and calling on the gods as a community. Therefore, you must find your Heathen kindred and become part of it.

Also, the more you connect with other Pagans, the more you learn about your faith and the deeper your beliefs get. Being part of a kindred is immensely useful in your research about your religion. Moreover, when other believers share their experiences with you, you will realize how similar these experiences are to your own.

It gives you a sense of identity and makes you realize and accept the presence of gods and deities all around you. You can counter arguments about being crazy to believe in the existence of gods. You know and accept their existence without question because you know others have had the same experiences as you.

The fifth step you should follow diligently in Norse Paganism is to have fun. Again, it makes sense to be reminded that gods and goddesses are your friends and family. You don't have to pray to them to forgive your sins and cry your heart out. You can explain your problems to them as you would to a good friend or a trusting elderly relative in your family and seek their guidance and wisdom to help you scale through the problems you face.

Our gods want us to be humans and have fun, including eating, drinking, and partying. They want us to embrace our imperfections and learn from our mistakes and keep improving ourselves so that we can lead increasingly meaningful and fulfilling lives. Our gods do not call us sinners who should be punished as a form of repentance. They teach us to learn from our errors and to incorporate the lessons into our future.

Altar (Indoor Altars, Outdoor Altars)

There are probably as many modern theories of what an ancient Norse Ve or Hof (temple, holy place) looked like as there were ancient Norse temples. I've heard everything (with full scholarly accompaniment) from groves in the woods to constructing buildings that were the basis for the later Stave Churches of Scandinavia. In general, I think the multiplicity of descriptions indicates that people were of an open and practical mind about what should be present in a temple and what form it should take. Our modern practice tends to reflect this.

The first distinction we might make in our modern practice is between altars that people have in their homes and the setup of the rooms that we perform group rituals in. For rituals, we tend to use any place large enough to fit everyone into it. For aesthetic reasons, we try to mask the normal use of the room, which in the past has included such things as covering the television set with a cloth and moving some of the more obtrusive furniture out of the room. The other preparatory element that I can't recommend highly enough indoors is to line the room with candles and eliminate any artificial lights. The darkness isn't an important part of the religious elements of the ritual, but it gets rid of a lot of distractions.

The altar itself is a rather simple affair. We often use a small table for this purpose. There's no specific setup for an altar in Asatru, other than it should look pleasant and hold all the implements you will need during the ritual. If you want to get fancy, you can symbolize the Gods, seasonally appropriate decorations, *etc.*

Asatru magic requires a limited number of tools—with the basics being an altar, dagger, and a cauldron. More complex magical practices require a long list of tools, including daggers, goblets, incense burners, candles, wands, runestones, and more. Also, special gems and other stones are used to entice and attract Elves and Dwarves. Some rituals also call for staff, horns and bells. For the beginners of Asatru magic, the first tool to be created or acquired is a sacred place dedicated to magical practices or an altar. The altar ideally sits on a stone slab, giving it an instrument to connect to the earth below. A wooden table or chest of drawers can also be used as an altar, preferably with a marble or a stone top. The entire altar does not have to be covered in stone, but the particular space used for magical rituals calls for a natural element such as stone or marble to amplify the spell's working and power.

Another magical tool in Asatru is a robe that is used only for magical practices. Wearing this robe whenever a ritual is practiced helps the subconscious mind of the practitioner to get into the realm of magic, working easily, leaving behind everyday life. Some Asatru practitioners also employ a special piece of jewelry such as an amulet or a necklace reserved only for magical practices just for this reason. Replicas of the Norse deity Thor's hammer is another special artifact placed on altars to condition the practitioner's mindset to focus on the magical realm of Asatru.

Not everyone has an altar, but many heathens have some kind of setup at home where they can focus their attention when they talk to the gods. An altar is made up of many different elements meaningful to the person who made it. Do not think of an altar as something that **must** contain certain items—it can contain exactly the objects you want and nothing else. An altar is a space you build or create for yourself, composed of only the items that make you feel comfortable. I have seen heathens use two kinds of altars: indoor altars and outdoor altars.

With an indoor altar, you have more options for putting objects on it. If, for instance, you are a person who feels closely attached to things such as heirlooms and you want to put them on your altar, they will be more secure on your indoor altar than an outdoor one. You also have the option to put elements on your indoor altar that would otherwise perish outdoors or be taken by animals.

Creating your indoor altar is rooted in how you intend to commune with the spirits. For instance, if runic meditation is something you like to do, it will be meaningful to place your set of runes on the altar. You can also place a picture, drawing, or painting of your favorite god or pictures of multiple gods. You can put rocks and plants there, too. If you like to interact with the gods and spirits through drink and food, you can have items on your altar for that. Drinking horns are very popular among Ásatrúar, especially ornately carved cow horns. You may also consider having a plate to put your offerings to the gods and spirits.

Many indoor altars are focused on ancestors rather than on gods and spirits. People place pictures of their family and deceased ancestors on the altar. They hang items that used to belong to their loved ones on the altar, and in that way, the altar becomes a space in the home where you can communicate with your long-gone ancestors. Most heathens believe that the dead do not die. They live on in our memories, in our hearts, and our surroundings. That idea is more important than any "paradise" or death-realm beyond our living world because it means that our ancestors never abandon us.

In my house, we have a family altar, which combines the ancestors and important spirits of our combined families. We have important items on our altar, including pictures, which have belonged to our grandparents and great-grandparents. Aside from that, we have flowers and wooden carvings, ritual instruments that we use in ceremonies, gifts and offerings for the gods and spirits, and many more items. All in all, what you put on your altar comes down to how you want to communicate with the gods, spirits, and ancestors.

An outdoor altar is naturally different from an indoor one. Of course, not everyone lives somewhere that will allow for an outdoor altar, but those who do may opt for an outdoor altar. The benefit of an outdoor altar is that you can pour libations to the gods and spirits directly onto the ground. You can fashion a full space to be used only for ritual acts, and you can make it as beautiful as you want—for instance, as a part of your garden.

Some heathens who have the space for outdoor altars design a part of their property as a little grove with trees and sometimes a pond. Others have a large rock where they put objects for the gods and spirits. Others have an altar built of several larger and smaller rocks. Some like to mark off the area around their altar with a circle. Often, the circle is comprised of smaller rocks, wooden sticks, small fences, or ropes.

While the ancient stories do not describe indoor altars, some give indications of how sacred outdoor spaces were created. In the Icelandic sagas, they talk about the type of sacred site called a *vé*, a space marked off with *vébönd*, bonds, or chains attached to hazelnut sticks. In several stories, we also find descriptions of special rocks, boulders, ponds, lakes, and creeks, which were used as focus points for personal rituals.

Magic Rituals and the Moon

As you move forward in your Wiccan journey, learning to use your magic, you will discover that the Moon is greatly influential. While most people do not track the Moon's cycle, it is important that practicing Wiccans make it a point to tap into that cycle, connecting with the Moon daily. You have several ways of doing this—rituals, such as the ones that will be discussed later, greeting the Moon, or even just a few moments to reflect upon it.

When you tune into the Moon's cycle, you can tap into the Moon's natural energies that are dependent upon where it is within its cycle or which sign it is currently in. As you do this, you can start to employ the subtleties existing between the varying states of the Moon. This means, then, that you can start to change when you choose to engage in your rituals, ensuring that you are always using the energies in the world around you to their fullest potentials, enhancing your magic.

Most people who are new to magic aren't in the habit of paying attention to the moon's rhythms as it orbits the Earth. If this is you, you might want to think about adopting a routine to connect to the moon daily. It could be as simple as a silent greeting or with a formal ritual.

Figure out where the moon is at and acknowledge this as a part of your practice daily. You will be able to find a full moon schedule online. This can help you become more in tune with the subtle differences during the lunar phases. From the new moon to the full moon, from the dark moon, and back to the new moon again, this never-ending moon cycle gives you many opportunities to get tuned into both the moon's and the world's energies to enhance your spells.

Phases of the Moon

Moon and Asatru magic have a deep connection to each other. Many magical rituals need to happen during a certain phase of the moon. For example, if the ritual calls for decreasing or removing a certain problem, it often takes place in the time after the Full Moon until the New Moon when the moon is in the waning phase. The night of the full moon is considered the most powerful time for casting spells and practicing magical rituals, just like many religions that are closer to nature in their essence. Interestingly, when looking at Asatru magic through a modern lens, there is logical reasoning behind the belief that the magical power of nature heightens during the full moon. It is a known fact that the tides of the ocean are affected by the moon. Since the human body and most of the natural elements are made largely of water, their energy can be affected by the Moon and its phases.

Mainstream culture tends to laugh off the notion of Moon-influenced feelings and behavior, but, as we have previously stated, the Moon does have effects on people and animals. This tends to be most obvious during the days surrounding the Full Moon, when we notice unusual behavior in our pets or children or feel ourselves to be abnormally "moody."

But while you may already be aware that the "Full Moon effect" is not a myth, you may not realize that *all* phases of the Moon's cycle influence us on some level, however subtle it may be for those who aren't yet attuned to lunar energy.

The way you respond to the Moon's energy will depend on many factors, including diet and exercise patterns, as well as influences in your astrological birth chart. Indeed, everyone's relationship with the Moon's cycle is unique, but if you start paying close attention to how you think and feel during each phase, you'll understand better how these rhythms affect your power. Then you can use these discoveries to strengthen your magical abilities.

What does the Moon's energy have to do with magic? As multi-sensory beings, we are constantly interacting with unseen energies coming from every direction—from other people, from media, from the food we eat, and the buildings we spend our days and nights in. Everything we interact with affects our energetic makeup.

We tend to focus on what we experience through our five physical senses—sight, sound, touch, taste, and smell. But our sixth sense—intuition—is the most crucial mode of perception when it comes to magic. The energy of the Moon is tailor-made for interacting with the energy of our intuition, which is also feminine, receptive, and magnetic.

When we consciously connect with lunar energy, we are opening up our capacity to channel that force into drawing what we desire and releasing what we don't want from our lives. When we do so in conscious harmony with the energetic rhythms of the Moon's cycle, we can truly amplify the power of our magical work.

Rituals for Full Moon Worship

Nights marked by the full moon are filled with magic and mystery. The light of the full moon bathes everything on earth in a strangely eerie glow. Sometimes it is almost as bright outside as it is during the daylight hours. Many Wiccans will celebrate the nights of the full moon with a specific monthly ritual known as an Esbat ritual. The rituals performed are specific to the particular Esbat. They are normally performed with a coven, but the elements can be tailored to individual practice.

Full Moon Ceremony for Spring

When spring finally arrives, everything feels different. There is a whispered promise of warmth and softness in the air, a new freshness, even in the days when the wind is still chilly and damp. New growth and new life are evident everywhere. The full moon of spring is a time of magic. During spring, there is an opportunity for abundance and fertility, growth, and rebirth. No matter which spring moon you are celebrating the element of Water is the focus of the lunar cycles of Spring.

Water is a source of life on earth. It can be used to purify, cleanse, and heal, but it can also be used to destroy life on earth. For our ancestors, the local spring or well was a place of magic where people gathered to talk, exchange information, gather water for home use, and bathe. We honor Water during any celebration of the Full Moon during Spring.

You will need to arrange your altar in an appropriate way for the Spring season. You will decorate with items that represent Spring, such as seed packets, flowers from the garden, or new sprigs from bushes. You will need a large empty bowl and a small bowl of water. If other people are participating in this ritual with you, then ask them to bring their small glass or jar of water from a special place to them. You will also need one freshly cut flower. If there is no one to be found, then a flowering cutting from a tree or a bush will work.

If you usually begin your rituals by casting a circle as part of your tradition, then you will do that now. And remember that this ritual can be used by an individual, a small group, or a full-sized coven. If you are performing a solitary ritual then you will act as the High Priestess. She is the one who will perform all the elements of the ritual.

Hold the small bowl of water in your hands and point it toward the sky as you face the Moon. Repeat these words:

The Moon lights our darkness

She lights our minds, our souls, and our worlds

She is ever constant and ever changing

The water that she moves with her cycles nourishes and cleanses us

It brings life to us

We create this sacred space with the divine energy of this sacred element Water

Hold the bowl of water in one hand and the cut flower in the other hand. Dip the petals of the flower into the water and use the water collected on the petals to sprinkle the ground as you walk in the shape of a circle. When you have created the circle, then set the bowl of water on the altar and chant these words:

Spring has come and brought us new life

The early morns are sunny and bright

The afternoon rains bring water and life

The water gives life to the new life growing around us

We welcome this water that has come from the universe

If others are participating in this ritual with you, then you will now take the large empty bowl and go to each participant, in turn, to allow them to add their water to the bowl. Let each person tell where they gathered the water and what makes it special to them. When everyone else has added their water to the bowl, then stir the water with the stem of the cut flower, allowing all of the waters to mix as you say:

The water comes together with the power of the Moon above

We grow with her power

In light, in energy, in love

Then use the bowl of blended water to anoint the forehead of each person with whatever symbol your tradition uses. If your group does not have a special symbol, then use something to symbolize the Full Moon while saying *"The light of the Full Moon will guide you with wisdom and light in the cycle that comes now."*

Now spend a few minutes in quiet meditation on the Water and the power it will bring to you. Think about its power to change everything in its path, how it ebbs and flows through the world. Imagine how water can bring life or destroy it. Think about how your body is connected to the moving tides of Water and how the power of the Water will bring strength to you. After a few minutes of quiet meditation, close the circle and end the ritual. Now take the time to enjoy a bit of ale and cakes or something similar like wine and crackers or juice and cookies, and if you are with a group, enjoy a bit of fellowship.

Full Moon Ceremony for Summer

The months of June, July, and August are the months when you should perform a ritual to honor the Summer Full Moon. This ritual is made for a small group, but it can be expanded to fit the needs of a full coven or performed by an individual.

The long, beautiful evenings of summer are perfect for outdoor rituals, especially after dark, when the Full Moon is bathing you with her light. If you are doing a group ritual, ask everyone to bring something to put on the altar that represents summer and its warmth. Your altar decorations should include short pillar candles in appropriate summer colors, fresh flowers or herbs, things that symbolize the sun, freshly ripened fruits, and something to represent cakes and ale. Remember, the food offering does not need to be alcoholic, so lemonade and sugar cookies would work just as well and would serve to symbolize the freshness and lightness of the summer months.

If this celebration is a group ritual, then several people will have roles to play. If you are doing an individual ritual, then you will complete all of the parts yourself. Cast your circle with whatever method you would like to use. Then you will call all of the four quarters. Someone (or you) will stand on the north side of the circle while holding a green candle. Light the candle and hold it high as though you are offering it to the sky. Repeat these words:

I welcome the powers of Earth to this circle

The heat of the Sun has warmed us and prepared our bounty

For a fruitful harvest

Set the green candle on the altar in the North position and leave it lit.

Then you will light the yellow candle and stand in the East and hold the candle to the sky while saying:

I welcome the powers of the Air to this circle

In this season of light and growth

May the Air and wind always bring us togetherness and fruitfulness.

Place the yellow candle on the altar, still lit, in the East position. Then light the red candle and hold it upward to the sky while saying these words:

Welcome powers of Fire to this circle

Light our way tonight with the light from the Full Moon

As the Sun lights our lives in the day

Then place the lighted red candle on the altar in the south position. Finally, light the blue candle and stand in the West, offering the candle to the sky while repeating this chant:

This circle welcomes the power of Water

Summer may dry and parch the earth with her heat

But the Water will bring the rains again to bring us life

Place the blue candle on the altar in the west position and then you, along with the group if you have one, will repeat this blessing:

By the light of the Moon, we gather together

We rejoice in the beauty of this season, and we celebrate

May we ever receive life and fertility, prosperity and abundance, compassion and love

With each turn of the Wheel, lighted by the Moon above

Now the circle will share the cakes and ale and tell one another a story about Summer and what it means to them. If you are performing a solitary ritual, then spend a few minutes meditating on Summer and its meaning in your life. Think of the bounty you have already received this year and what is to come. If you have a spell to cast or another ritual to perform, then you must do that now. If not, then it is time to close the circle.

Full Moon Ceremony for Autumn

September, October, and November are the months of Autumn when you will perform the Autumn ritual for the Full Moon. While this particular ritual is intended for a small group, it can easily be done solo or with a large coven. If possible, you should perform this ritual outside during the Full Moon. Autumn nights are generally cool and crisp with just a touch of the coming winter to remind you; so, the evenings under the light of the Moon should be pleasant. If you are doing this ritual with a group, then ask everyone to bring a small item that they will put on the altar, something that makes them think of Autumn. If you are decorating the altar yourself, then you might use black or orange cloths, newly picked apples; pumpkins, squashes, or gourds; red or yellow leaves; and some stalks of wheat or another grain from the last harvest. The cakes and ale can easily be represented by apple cider and pumpkin spice cookies.

Use the appropriately colored candles to call the quarters after you cast the circle. Beginning in the North, you will say:

Welcome to this circle, powers of Earth

May the harvest be bountiful

May you bless us with plenty

For the South, you will say:

Welcome to this circle power of Air

Bring us knowledge and wisdom with your changing winds

And bounty and abundance in this season

And the last candle will be lighted to call in the West, and you will repeat these words:

Welcome Water to this circle

Bring your powers to wash away the last heat of summer

Bring us the coming chill

Then the group (or you) will give this blessing:

The light of the Moon calls us to gather

We celebrate this season, and we rejoice in its power

May it bring us abundance and prosperity in all our harvests

With the power from the Moon above

Now enjoy the cakes and ale and talk about, or meditate on, just exactly what is hoped for in the coming months and how the year has gone so far. Think of the things that you plan to work on in the upcoming months since the bulk of the work for the year is done. What are your plans? If you are planning to cast a spell or you have another ritual to perform, you must do it now. If not, then you must close the circle and end the ritual.

Full Moon Ritual for Winter

The Full Moon ritual for winter is more of a private ritual, although you can easily create a ritual to perform with a small group or a coven. The end of the year is a time for reflecting on the year past and making plans for the upcoming year. What worked for you this year? What do you feel you will need to change in the next year?

The days are getting shorter, and the nights are long and cold. It may be too cold to perform a ritual outside or too rainy or snowy. It is perfectly acceptable to perform your ritual inside. Decorate your altar in the colors of the season which are black, red, and white. Lay fir or pine tree branches or bits of holly around your altar. Set out bowls of cinnamon, holly, and mistletoe. Even though this season is one of darkness, the winter solstice marks the return of the light, so you can also celebrate the element of Fire by lighting incense in the appropriate scent.

The idea of the ritual this time of the year is personal cleansing. Light some candles and some pine or cinnamon incense. Put on some soft seasonal music. Start small, with a drawer or a container in the closet. Get rid of the objects you have not touched in six months, no longer fit you or are not your style preference anymore, or that just do not make you happy any longer. Getting rid of physical clutter will make the spaces around you feel larger and more accommodating. Set aside the items you want to donate and say a blessing over them.

Once you have purged the unwanted items from your home, you should smudge your house to cleanse it. Use mistletoe, pine needs, sweetgrass, or sage as your smudge tool. Either use incense or put loose herbs in a heatproof bowl and light them on fire. Let the smoke begin to rise and start at the front door with your smudging ritual. You can use this verse or one similar to it; you can even write your own.

Cleanse my home, cleanse my space

Fill it with peace and joy and grace

Negative thoughts do not belong

Send them away, and they shall be gone

Bring to this house light and love

Gifts from the Goddess above

You can also perform a ritual to honor the Goddess. First, decorate your altar using cloths in the seasonal colors of red, green, white, and gold. Set out some incense in the holiday scents of myrrh, cinnamon, and frankincense. Set out two candles in white, green, red, or gold. If you usually start your rituals by casting a circle, then do it now, but it is not mandatory. Light the first candle and repeat this verse:

This is the longest night of the year, the night of the Solstice

The Wheel keeps turning and will soon return the Sun to us

New life will begin on Earth as the Goddess blesses her children

Now light the second candle and repeat this verse:

Tonight, I celebrate the Winter Solstice in the season of the winter Goddess

The Sun will be reborn, and the light will return to earth

As I give thanks and honor for the eternal cycles

Now light the incense and turn on any holiday lighting that may be decorating your home. Light any other candles you may have decorating your altar or your home. Return to your altar and lift your hands to the sky and repeat this chant:

This night I honor the Mother, the Goddess, who rules over this season

I thank the Goddess for her many gifts this year

I pray she will continue to bless me in the coming year

I send my prayers to you, oh Goddess

Now enjoy some cakes and ale and think about what changes you might like to make in your life during the next year. What new seeds do you intend to plant in the hopes that they will grow? What new plans do you have for your growth and development when the light returns to the earth? When you feel ready, you can finish the ceremony by closing the circle if you opened one and gently snuffing out the candles.

Chapter 4: Types of Asatru Magic

When it comes to rituals and rites, the Norse people had many of them; most were devoted to the practice and inclusion of Norse magic. There was no organized religion; instead, there was a spiritual practice deeply attached to magic. Because of their use, its symbols were sacred and bound to meaning for society as a whole. At the same time, they were also individualized by each community and each family.

Magical healers, though often revered, were also outcasts. No organization supported them in the strictest sense. So, when Christianity did come along, it was not at all uncommon to have a mix of Old Norse magic practiced side-by-side with this new religion. These practices were identified simply as the old and the new.

Old Norse magic-based faith was called "forn sidr," which means ancient custom; Christianity was referred to as the new custom or "nyr sidr." One could say that both involved sacred acts, rituals, and worship of higher powers. These were not that different from each other to the Norse people.

Old Norse magic and culture were often borrowed and transformed. Ideas, including those about the importance of magic rituals, reached the Germanic tribes over time and across great stretches of land so that traditions and incantations and stories and myths were transformed as they passed through these distances.

Norse magic is infused with this kind of heterogeneous assimilation, but it is also firmly rooted in the land and the people themselves. Some celebrations were individualized because of this. This refers to the idea of sacrifice or blot, as well as feast days and celebrations that included alcoholic drinks such as mead and food such as meat from animals who were sacrificed to the gods.

Both celebration and sacrifice often played out on specific seasons or were used to celebrate or improve fertility, ensure success in battle, or a good harvest. They were also used to ensure happy births, strong marriages, peaceful burials, and transitions to the afterlife. They were often customized specifically for particular communities or individuals.

Naturally, everything we know about rituals and practices from this time is also colored through the lens of the sweep of Christianity and the belief by newly minted Christians that the rituals of the Norse people were marked by superstition or involved worshipping demons. However, much of what we're highlighting here is based on archaeological evidence, including that of the runic alphabet.

When it comes to this, some things are easy to refute, while others seem fairly easy to acknowledge and understand. In many cases, it's almost certain that private and public rituals were both taking place and likely mirrored each other. Let's start with a look at the most common and likely rituals.

In the Old Norse world, the spoken word had strong powers. They believed that anything spoken had great power and influence in their lives. Once something was said, whatever happened afterward couldn't be changed, and they could never take back what was said. They believed that words made the reality and not that reality made words. It's not that words reflect a person's perception of the world, but, instead, a person's experience and understanding of the world are affected by the things their language demands. Saying what you think was unheard of because they believed once it was said; it would change the course of reality.

Each rune was a representation of a phoneme, which is the smallest unit of sound, making it a visual form of a phoneme.

Many linguists don't look at the relationships between the meaning of a word and the sound of the word. Some scholars embrace this belief, which is called phonosemantics. This means that there is a connection between the sound a word makes and its meaning. Another way to look at this is the fact that each phoneme had its meaning. For example, look at the work thorn. It is built by the phonemes "th", "o", "r", and "n".

The phonosemantic view ties back into the belief that words can create a reality and not reality forming words. Since runes are a drawing of phonemes, that causes them to bring about the creative power of language into a visual system. Rune's second meaning is a letter; its first is secret. This can be seen in the story where Odin discovered the Runes. If they weren't a secret, he wouldn't have had to go through what he did to discover them.

The runes could be used by both nonhumans and humankind. This gave the two a way to communicate with each other and provided them with the basis of many magical acts.

Magic could be used to bring calamitous curses on one's enemies, as well as to provide protection in battle, increase fertility in both people and the land on which they lived. But one of its most important uses was perhaps healing. Many Old Norse spells revolved around healing.

In part, in Old Norse communities, sickness and strife required some sort of categorization just to deal with them.

Regardless of what being was housing these evil spirits, the solution was viewed in terms of expelling them. Much as Christians prayed for their health, the Old Norse often called upon Thor for help.

Herbs and Potions

Archaeobotany had brought up some very interesting findings when it came to the use of plants for healing and magic. The Norse used different plants to remove infection or pain, or a combination of poisonous plants and alcoholic meads that would allow the person to slip into a trance and remove themselves from their physical body to connect to the spirit realm. Each god had an herb that was connected to their theme, which would allow one to interact with this deity when the plant was used for healing, cooking, or potions, called the magical union.

Here are some of the most common plants used at the time:

- Henbane was used in smoking or drinking, which activated its extremely toxic properties, assisting in the arrival of a trance state.

- Mugwort was used as a diuretic in the household and rituals for divination.

- Bog Myrtle or Sweet Gale was used as a flavoring additive to many brews and as an antiseptic ointment.

- Meadowsweet was used as a cure for headaches or to alleviate indigestion.

- The Elm plant was used as a magical connection to the Alfheim realm and to carry love spells and other charms into the afterworld.

Many other plants were used in conjunction with rituals as well as their household use. Some connected to the dead and ancestors, and some to love and the living.

Sacred Numbers

In paganism, numbers were often recycled to keep their relevance in each story told. In Norse mythology, we see the numbers three and nine. These numbers reflect in the **Poetic Edda** and the Icelandic Sagas.

The number three is portrayed in many ways:

- Ymir, Búri, and the cow, Audhumla, are the three original beings.

- There are three Norns.

- There are three sacred wells.

- Before Ragnarök has its time, three long winters will ensue.

- Odin sacrificed himself three times at the Yggdrasil tree in search of the runes.

- Many of the sacred possessions of the gods come in three.

The number nine is portrayed in many ways as well:

- There are nine worlds supported by Yggdrasil.

- Odin hangs from the branches of Yggdrasil for nine days and nights.

- The nine mothers of Heimdallr.

- The great feast and sacrifice in Uppsala occur every nine years.

- Odin's golden ring Draupnir releases nine golden drops every nine nights.

- Freyr is required to wait nine nights before he can consummate his love for giantess Gerðr.

Knot Work

Designed to reduce fever, pain, or swelling and ease labor during childbirth, knot work, including both tying and untying knots, was one of the facets of healing magic the Old Norse employed. It was also used to protect against snakebites. The use of knots to ease childbirth persisted long after Norse magic disappeared after the sweep of Christianity into the region. Some evidence suggests that Freya's followers, along with being magic practitioners, were also called up to assist in childbirth through midwifery.

Sometimes, instead of physical knots, verbal spells that mimicked them were used. A runic word was written down about an ailment, and repeatedly written until only a single letter remained.

Spirit Worlds Wights

Landvættir were the spirits and wights of the land and the natural places surrounding Iceland.

People would often worship and ask for advice in rocks, woods, and waterfalls, as the wights controlled the life of the land, its fertility, and health. Some stories implied that they were already there before the Norse settled, like in the Saga of King Olaf Tryggvason in the **Heimskringla.** King Harald Bluetooth wanted to invade Iceland, but before he could, he needed a wizard to send out his spirit to scout for locations where it would be easy to infiltrate the land.

<u>Útiseta</u>

This was a practice of clarity. Sitting out the night on crossways was not only for invoking spirits and deities to reveal secrets or counsel but also to meditate and prepare one's energy for other more strenuous practices later.

It required sitting in darkness in nature, covered in a cloak or blanket, and fasting for many days, as Útiseta means "powering down" or "the act of sitting out" to provoke spirits. The communication received from the outside, such as sounds, smells, and feelings grounded the person and clarified their minds so they may hear the spirits around them. The encounter between pupil and spiritual teacher was the goal, looking for answers in the wilderness within and without. Depending on the knowledge you seek, you would invoke the assistance of Odin, Freyja, or Thor.

Totemism

The Norse Kingdoms frequently partook in the practice of totemism. This is the spiritual relationship between humans and different types of animals or plants. The totem is considered the guardian or ancestor of the human whom it is connected to and overlaps the human self—meaning that if the owner died, so did the totem.

Before Christianization, their worldview of this state of being and connection to the natural world was separated into two factions, as explained below.

The Fylgjur

These were the personal animal spirits of individuals assigned to them at birth. *Fylgjur* means 'follower' in Old Norse; therefore, we can understand it as a companion that has a direct correlation to the health of the owner.

The sagas talk about animals such as cats, dogs, foxes, wolves, birds of prey, and mice. Each person's character will be affected by the inherent character of the animal they are connected to. The character of a leader would have the untamed nature of the fox, deer, eagle, or lion, whereas the tame nature of a woman, for example, would be that of a boar, ox, or goat. If you were of noble descent, it was a bear; if you were of a violent person, it was a wolf, and so on.

Ancestor Worship

Another ritual was worshiping one's ancestors, which was deemed especially important because people believed that deceased ancestors could still influence or affect the life of their descendants. While they were regarded as having left the life that the living walked in, they were thought to still be living their afterlives within Norse cosmology, depending on how they had died. When treated to the respect they deserved through proper rituals, they could bless the living and help assure their prosperity and happiness; if not, they could curse them, bring them a bad fortune, or even summon evil elves to work against them.

Part of the ritual worshiping of ancestors rested on items placed within the burial mounds. These objects were considered sacred. Graves were positioned close to family homes, as ancestors were thought to protect the dwelling and its inhabitants. In a more practical sense, this also prevented the looting of graves.

Land Wight Worship

Land wights were spiritual beings thought to protect areas of land. As such, they were to be respected. Many rules were established so that people could avoid having any conflicts with them. They could be frightened away, which would bring bad luck. In old Norse, they were called "landvættir," or the spirits that dwell in a place or land feature. They were thought to have power and influence over the land and its wellbeing, as well as people who lived or traveled through it. They would either bless or curse people.

Wights protected the land and were intolerant of any mistreatment or dishonor to it or them. Great care was taken to maintain and draw a wight's favor and not to frighten it away. There is a connection between the wights and the gods, the elves, dwarves, and giants.

Women were most often in charge of caring for land wights, placing and maintaining offerings of food and drink near locations such as wooded areas and water sources where wights were said to live. Seid, galdr, and the use of runes were all important elements of Norse rituals, used to contact deities and ancestors, for divination and omen interpretation, as well as to bless and curse.

Runes were a big part of just about any ritual, whether used for casting lots or as symbols. It is not known which particular runes were attributed to which rituals or events.

The closest we can come to understanding or glimpsing rituals comes from more recent history and is based on sagas about or by Scandinavian people. In one such account, Odin required a sacrifice for a good year at the start of winter, another for rebirth in midwinter, and yet another for victory during summer.

The dead were to be cremated, ashes spread at sea, or buried in the ground. The gravesites and burial mounds themselves add credence to the stories in the sagas, acknowledging them. It is only through a combination of both archeological references and written sources that we can form an idea of which rituals were used in Norse magic, both privately and publicly.

The names of specific locations or the use of symbols or runes identifying them also offer insight into these rituals. Several locales translate to contemporary Scandinavian languages as "Thor's Temple," for example. Areas consecrated in some form of ritual were identified with the term "ve," which means the location was one of the areas where special rules applied.

Ritual Spells

Considered the most active of healing spells, ritual magic, or sympathetic magic is the performance of an action or incantation over an object to make or cause a reaction for the patient. When invoking a ritual spell to cure a broken leg or ongoing back pain, the practitioner might use sticks to stand in for the afflicted limb, binding them, striking them, or slashing them while using a ritual question and answer session aimed to transfer the location or source of the illness or injury to the piece of wood where it can be more easily vanquished.

All of these different types of magic, from ritual/sympathetic magic to herbal healing to runic symbols, were used to eradicate disease or injury that was viewed as created or caused by evil spirits and trolls. Thor was often called upon to facilitate the healing process.

One of the first steps in creating the best healing regimen was divination, usually by casting runes, to identify what was causing the illness.

Sung runes, as well as written words, were considered especially useful. The most common runes used, whether spoken, sung, or invoked in writing were thurisaz, nauthiz, isa, raidho, and ansuz.

If written, rune spells were commonly attached to a patient's body, placed under a pillow, or consumed by the patient. It was also common to bind the evil spirit to a rock, stick, or another object of containment or banish it elsewhere so that it could not return and harm the patient again.

Spells used in Norse magic each contained a stave, a symbol that identified the runes laid out to cast that spell. Runes, as previously mentioned, were often carved on rock or wood and were viewed as a useful alphabet and a component of magic spells. The spells revealed that the runes themselves were powerful vehicles for magic.

Along with rituals, and as a part of their practice, spells were an important aspect of Norse magic, which practitioners needed to know accurately. A misinterpretation could lead to a curse instead of a blessing, losing an important battle, or poor harvests, among other things.

A strong element of any Norse magic is, of course, runes. Runic magic could be cast from rune stones or sung and chanted in the practice of galdr.

Breath Work

Some practices are the same across cultures. The importance of breathwork as a healing property is an intrinsic part of meditation and yoga. It's often used in kundalini yoga and yoga nidra. The Old

Norse believed, and rightfully so, that the human breath itself had the power to heal.

This was related to the belief that when a völva was practicing magic and entered a trance, their souls left their bodies. Once separated, the soul could commune with other souls and receive information about healing. Breathing could also be used to expel illness, nausea, or bad energy. (Heide, 2006)

Runes

Using the runic alphabet and singing runic incantations was a major aspect of healing spells. Even spells involving herbs or objects usually incorporated some kind of runic language along with them. Both galdr and seiðr frequently used language spells. Runes were carved into objects and kept by an afflicted person's bed. Symbols that were wearable were given to someone who was ill. There were engraved and wearable amulets, and there were rune sticks. To use the latter, a carved stick was tied to the body of an ailing person. The stick was specifically placed where the ailment existed or was believed to be. That could mean a stick was placed on a burn or wound, on a distended stomach, or over a rash. Sticks or jewelry were often inscribed with a specific runic word or words and other times with runes used as symbols rather than forming actual words.

Herbal Healing

While runic incantations for healing might focus more on prayer, like chanting or spiritual assistance, and written runic instructions are considered less useful today, herbs were a potent medicinal cure then. And they are still now, even if the intent was originally for the herbs to conjure the magic of healing rather than to offer a holistic alternative to modern Western medicine. And who is to say that they do not? The powerful healing aspect of herbs was increased by the chanting or singing of galdr incantations or songs over them while they were harvested and dried and when they were given to a patient.

Along with being administered to humans, domestic animals also were often given herbs as part of a magic-based veterinary treatment. Deeply important to survival on a farmstead, domestic animals often received the same treatments that humans did.

Herbal medicine and magic, doctoring, midwifery, and magical practice all went hand in hand. In many cases, herbal concoctions can provide healing even today in the era of mass-produced pharmaceuticals.

Using Seidr and Galdr

Seidr spells were not used so much for healing as they were to identify the cause of an illness or the location of a wound within the body. Many spells began with an incantation about being found. (Hyacinth Halcyon, 2016)

Rune casting could also be used to foretell or uncover the cause of an illness and provide protective spells to end it.

Once an actual illness was found or diagnosed, then the evil spirit behind the illness could be cast out through a spell or chant, or the use of other magical properties.

Magical Stones and Crystals

Along with herbs, many stones and crystals were used for healing. In some cases, crystals were crushed and applied to the skin or even consumed through the mouth.

Healing crystals are connected to the seven chakras or energy centers within the body: the crown of the head, the third eye, the throat, the heart, the solar plexus, the sacral chakra, and the root of the body. Sometimes heat or vibrations can be felt when using the stones. Some stones were perceived as being more helpful than others.

- Dwarf stone or dvergarsteinar refers to polished crystals whose reflective light properties were used for healing. Crystals were also, as mentioned in an earlier chapter, often used for spindles and in the making of woven garments and textile-based spells.

- Lyfsteinar, the "life stone" or "cure stone" comes from the word "lyfja" which means to heal. The stones were often attached to swords or shields and were said to protect the bearer or heal them from wounds. (Hyacinth Halcyon, 2016)

- Another often used stone was jorelo. This brown stone was used to treat sores or boils. It was placed in a bowl of milk, and then the milk was rubbed on the sores.

- Skøtlo stones were used to prevent miscarriages. They are linked to the healing attributes of Thor.

- Fluorite, amethyst, and selenite also have healing properties and were used by placing them near or on a sick person's body.

Amulet and rune sticks could also employ crystals or stones or accompany them. As mentioned earlier, healing spells or symbols were often attached to the afflicted person's body via amulet or rune stick inscription. In some cases, those types of woods considered better suited to healing, such as the ash, which is also associated with the great tree of life, were used to create healing rune sticks.

Household and Human Fluids Magic

The old Norse, at times, let blood flow from cuts made to the body. The ill person would then consume their own blood. Spit was often expelled from the body three times. This process was usually performed at the conclusion of a spell.

Numerous households had magicians, most of which were housewives. The ladies used distaffs and spindles to tell fortune, which is why spinning was considered significant in their households. The spinners with proficient skills were blessed with good fortune and luck, whereas the ones who mishandled or lost the ability to use a distaff were cursed with bad luck and suffered for the entire year. This is why most women took spinning extremely seriously and predetermined their family's luck. It is believed that the spinning goddesses took charge and visited each household to determine the quality of tools used by the housewives, after which their fate was decided and altered.

Such instances of the changing fates of children and families have been regularly mentioned in the Norse accounts. One such tale is named "Märchen of Sleeping Beauty," in which persistent spinning is used to alter a child's fate now and then. This tale had a major impact on all housewives and inculcated the belief of piercing their fingers with a sharp object to draw blood during pregnancy, preferably in the seventh month. A wooden piece was also assembled and adorned with protective symbols to secure the pregnant women from evil spirits.

Furthermore, the ladies spun three linen threads with different shades of black, red, and white that were used for different purposes once the baby was born. While the black thread was burned with the wooden piece to ward off evil spirits and curses, the red thread was tied around the newborn's hand for protection. The white thread was tied to the baby's umbilical cord. These instances explain the significance of the act of spinning and protective threads in households. Women with magical powers or those who could chant powerful mantras used their ability to protect their household and newborns.

While the art of spinning was majorly used for noble causes, some even used it to harm others. The mothers of Old Norse households would often sense lingering danger around their children and used their weaving skills to make protective shirts for them. The sons who went to war were given magically woven Raven Banners that turned black on the battlefield when danger approached the warriors. These banners were mostly woven by the warriors' sisters and mothers to strengthen their protection. Shades of blue and red were prioritized among all colors due to their magical potency. Red was used in healing and medical applications.

From gods to humans, almost all souls in the Norse universe possessed the ability to acquire and practice magical skills. As previously stated, magic was prevalent in both genders but was more prominent in women. It was regarded as women's art and was inextricably linked to their livelihood. However, some men delved deeper and acquired magical powers who were later questioned about their manhood and shamed by society. Regardless, Norse magic and rituals have since been an intriguing topic that marks significant events in the Norse universe. It is believed that a few people still practice or are trying to acquire ancient Norse magical skills.

Chapter 5: Tools of Asatru Magic

Tools Used in Old Norse Magic

Mjolnir

It was made by Odin and presented to Thor. It was forged from two parts: the forging hammer (Mjolnir) and the handle (leggings). The forging hammer has the power of lightning in its head. The handle is decorated with a snake or dragon figure and has a hidden compartment stored in the most powerful spell, used by Odin himself. Through this spell, it's possible to cast four magical spells simultaneously.

Thor used the Mjolnir hammer to protect the gods from evil spirits or prevent the world's destruction. He's been seen battling giants with it, but he never uses it against humans because he hates war and bloodshed. It was also used by Thor whenever he wanted to punish someone who sinned against him or his friends. When not in use, the Mjolnir hammer is kept in a container under Odin's throne in Valhalla.

Gleipnir

Loki's binding cord Gleipnir is a special sort of ribbon which can be used either to bind someone or release them. It was made by the dwarfs and given to the gods for them to bind Loki in an attempt to stop him from causing mischief.

It is made from the hair of a mare, which was said to have been used in some way by every individual creature on earth, some with positive and others with negative attributes. Each hair has the power to bind or release any creature that it touches. Gleipnir translates as 'the binding one.'

Gram

Odin is often described wielding his sword Gram in battles with other gods. It has a golden hilt with black runes inscribed on it that would be unlocked only when drawn by someone destined to defeat Odin himself. Gram would then glow in the hands of its rightful owner.

Gram was a gift to Odin from the giant Mímir, and this weapon gave him victory in many battles. As well as being Odin's sword, it was also his symbol of power, and he carried it into battle with him. Odin used his sword in duels against his brothers Vili and Vé. In some versions of the mythic battle, Odin loses his eye which was later replaced by a blood-red iris to reflect the pain he felt.

It was also used in fights with Hoenir and Loki, who tricked it out of Odin's grasp by disguising their hands as Freya's. The sword Gram can never be broken but will break any other sword that it strikes against. It is also known as "Aegir's-bane," "Aegir" being

Odin's father, the sea god, and its stabbing ability made it his weapon of choice.

Gungnir

Gungnir, the Spear of Destiny, has been in Odin's possession since the beginning of time. It was born out of a piece of wood that fell from Yggdrasil, the tree of life containing and connecting the nine worlds. Under orders from Odin, Heimdall, the watchman of the gods, planted that piece of wood on Midgard (Earth), and sorcery made it grow into an immense tree to which Heimdall gave his blood. After Gungnir, the spear was born, runes were carved into it so nobody could lift it and harm Odin.

Gungnir is the symbol of Odin's power, which he uses to protect the gods. Odin used the spear to punish criminals and evil spirits that attacked Asgard. In case of a war against humans, Gungnir was launched in front of the gods, and its divine power would destroy all evil warriors. Gungnir is kept in a metal ring (to which no magic can be applied) where none but Odin can touch it or see it.

Dainsleif

Dainsleif is the sword that Thor used to punish criminals and evil spirits. It was forged by dwarves, using a portion of Yggdrasil's heart. It had been in Thor's possession since the beginning of time and was never lost or stolen. Dainsleif is considered to be one of the most powerful weapons in Asgard. It's easily recognizable because its blade is as wide as three men.

These magical weapons have become part of our myths and legends and inspire many works of fiction. They are also a powerful representation of the Norse people's culture and beliefs. In many ways, these weapons embody the strengths and weaknesses of the gods.

Modern Asatru Magic Tools

Sword

Common within ceremonial magic and traditional forms of Wicca, yet rarely seen outside of them, the sword is a masculine tool corresponding to either fire or air. It is a defensive tool used for banishing, commanding spirits, and casting the circle (an energetic construct used as part of delineating ritual space).

Bell

Associated with the element of air, the bell is used in various witchcraft traditions as a tool for cleansing and purification and banishing spirits and faeries. The tongue of the bell is sometimes viewed as masculine, while the bell itself is feminine.

Besom

A ritual broom used solely by witches, the besom is employed to remove unwanted energies from an area as part of cleansing rituals. It is associated with either fire or air and is sometimes leaped over as part of handfasting ceremonies.

Athame

A black-handled knife found within ceremonial magic and Wicca, the athame typically has a dull blade, as it is not used for physical cutting. It corresponds to either fire or air, depending on tradition, and is a primary tool used for directing energy.

Wand

Belonging to both ceremonial magic and Wicca, the wand is made from a living branch cut from a tree. Some traditions will modify the branch by embedding a metal rod within it, while others will inscribe symbols upon its surface. Aligned with either fire or air, the wand is a tool of invocation and evocation, used to draw energies and spirits. However, some witches have come to use the wand as an alternative to the athame.

Chalice or Cup

Corresponding to the water element, the chalice is a ritual cup found in both ceremonial magic and Wicca. It enjoys practical use in many Pagan traditions on occasions when a ritual beverage is shared among participants. Some traditions view it as a symbol of divine feminine energy.

Cauldron

A tool of transformation, change, and inspiration, the cauldron is rarely found outside witchcraft traditions and Druidry. It is associated with both fire and water and may be used to hold liquid water or actual flames as part of the ritual.

Pentacle

A small disc made of metal, stone, or wax, the pentacle is inscribed with various symbols, sometimes (but not always) including the symbol of the pentacle. It is a traditional tool of Wicca, used to represent the element of Earth and to consecrate tools and direct energy.

Staff

Found within various Pagan traditions, the staff is a large piece of wood, generally about the height of the person to whom it belongs. It may be carved or decorated. It corresponds to either the fire or the air element.

Candles

A versatile tool ubiquitous in Paganism, candles are used to represent the element of fire. However, they are more commonly used as a primary tool in magick, as representations of deities, focal points in magick and ritual, and luminaries for the altar.

Book of Shadows

Found within Wicca, a Book of Shadows is a personal book that contains all of the lore and rites of that particular Wiccan tradition up to the degree to which that individual has been initiated. It also includes personal lore and witchcraft material, such as documentation of spells, herb lore, and divinatory readings.

Crystals, Stones, and Minerals

A common component of magick, stones, and minerals—including salt—are used due to the intrinsic energies within them. Admittedly, many Pagans prefer the crystalline forms of minerals; however, many of these "crystals" have been cut and shaped, as they are not naturally found that way. From the animist perspective, the spirits within these stones can be spoken with, a relationship can be forged with them, and their help can be requested in magick.

Robe

Pagans of many traditions, especially clergy, will wear robes during ritual to represent the ritual's sacredness, adopt the necessary difference in mindset for the ritual, and denote their role. Outside of Druidry, where robes are traditionally white, there are few standards for what Pagan ritual wear or robes must look like.

Censer

A small dish for holding charcoal discs for smoldering incense, the censer is a practical tool that enjoys considerable use by many Pagans. Incense is a common component in ritual and magick. The censer is associated with the element of air. It is a tool of transference and movement.

Hammer

Found exclusively within Heathenry, the hammer is symbolic of Mjölnir and is used in ritual to convey blessings.

Stang

The stang is sometimes used interchangeably with the staff, but it is generally a tool found primarily within traditional witchcraft traditions (not to be confused with Wicca) and differs in that it has forked branches at the top (typically two, so that the stang resembles the letter Y) or features the skull of a horned animal at the top, such as a deer or goat, rather than possessing forking branches. It is a versatile tool used at the center of rituals, with the altar being built around and upon it. It represents the world tree and is also used within magick.

Crane Bag

A practical tool found in Druidry, the crane bag holds all other ritual tools, such as small instruments, divination tools, incense, and candles, as well as a lighter or matches, a utility knife, and maybe even the Druid's car keys.

Chapter 6: The Norse Paganism Today

The Asatru Association is an Icelandic religious formalized organization of Heathenry established on the First Day of Summer in 1972 by Sveinbjörn Beinteinsson, a farmer and poet. The First Day of Summer in Iceland is a national holiday and is celebrated on the first Thursday after April 18th annually. The Asatru Association was recognized and registered as a religious organization in 1973. The chief religious official or the highest office of the Asatru Association is referred to as "Allsherjargodi," an elected post.

The priests in Asatru are called Godi, and each Godi is given a congregation called godord to work with. While each godord is more or less connected to certain geographic regions, there is no compulsion to join any specific godord. You are free to join any congregation that you like.

The legal approval allowed the organization to conduct legally binding rituals and ceremonies as well as to collect a share of the church tax, which is imposed by the tax on religious congregations to run and manage churches and their employees. Sveinbjörn Beinteinsson led this organization from its inception in 1972 until he died in 1993. During his time, the membership of this organization did not exceed 100 people, and there was not much activity.

The second Allsherjargodi was Jörmundur Ingi Hansen, who led the organization from 1994 to 2002, and it was during this time that the Asatru Association witnessed considerable activity and growth. The third and current leader is the musician Hilmar Örn Hilmarsson, who took charge in 2003.

Asatru does not conform to a fixed religion, theology, or dogma. Each individual is free to have his or her own beliefs. For example, many Wiccan members are also members of the Asatru Association. The Asatru priests believe in a pantheistic perspective. The communal blot feast is the central ritual of Asatru. The priests also conduct naming ceremonies called gooar, weddings, funerals, coming of age, and other rituals too.

The worldwide map of Heathens is a great way to connect with other Heathens too. Here is a step-by-step of how you use this map. The website link is given later on.

Open the map from the link and zoom in to your area. Even if you don't find anyone very close to your home, you will likely find Heathens within driving distance of your place of residence.

Moreover, even if you don't find anyone close to where you live, you can contact many believers (even if they live far away). They are likely to connect you with someone they know who, perhaps, lives closer to you.

Don't forget to add yourself to the map. Someone in the future might find you and seek out your guidance. This is your way of making the path of Heathenry smoother for new entrants.

If you want something badly, the universe will find a way to bring it to you. Therefore, keep your desire to become an Asatru burning through self-learning and self-development. The more you delve deeper into yourself, the more your knowledge about the external world expands. Continue your efforts to connect with fellow believers. Sooner rather than later, you are likely to meet with such people and have a great community to rely on.

Norse Paganism in the Modern World

According to the Asatruars, Asatru is a revival of the ancient Norse Paganism beliefs. The word "revival" is key to fully understanding the nature of this religion in the modern world. Following the Christianization of Northern Europe, all that was left of Norse Paganism was the small number of people who could covertly practice their beliefs without getting found out. The religion had almost died out by the 12th Century. In the late 20th Century, some decided to rekindle the flame, choosing to reconnect with their ancestors' pre-Christian beliefs. In other words, Norse Paganism is not a modern creation but a revival of a religion that existed for centuries before.

An Asatruar's most distinguishing feature is their connection to themselves, their people, and nature. Most Asatruars have deep connections with their respective universes because they were taught to open up and embrace their spirituality. Since heathens are taught to see themselves as powerful beings equal to the Norse gods, they gradually gain the confidence needed to navigate their path in life.

Given the lack of a fixed dogma and the fact that many new believers converted to Norse Paganism from monotheistic religions, there are many interpretations of the Pagan texts and various understandings of several topics, such as how the gods interact with humans and whether or not the Vaettir are considered gods. With all of the differences, there is a sense of mutual respect and understanding of different points of view and interpretations. Asatru priests, on the other hand, are not believed to be inherently better than any other practitioner but rather as people who have a strong devotion to their religion.

The origin of Asatru is a fascinating story. It is almost unbelievable that this religion can survive centuries of Christianization behind hidden doors and then make its way out into the modern world centuries later. This only emphasizes the significance and weight of the connection between Norse Paganism and Norse identity. Asatru would not have emerged if there had not been a strong desire among modern peoples to reconnect with nature and their ancestors' beliefs. The only thing more intriguing is how religion has evolved to adapt to modern times. It is not only interesting from an academic standpoint, but it also demonstrates that Norse Paganism is an ever-changing set of concepts and beliefs, and therefore a living, breathing religion.

Asatru is based on Snorri Sturluson's Poetic and Prose Eddas, which were written in the 13th century. However, in contrast to systemic religions, there is no single indisputable source or concrete interpretation. Using the Eddas (texts and individual/group interpretations), folklore, and information passed down from generation to generation, believers have reconstructed Norse Paganism in the most authentic way possible. While some elements, such as blood sacrifices and tribe protection, have been modernized as humans have evolved socially, economically, and morally, the core intention behind all rituals and concepts has not evolved. The revival process was and is the delicate process of deconstructing and analyzing the Eddas in search for what lies at the center of the ancient Norse Pagans' beliefs and relationship with their Gods and spirits and their universe altogether.

Where to Find Fellow Believers

Here are some suggestions and recommendations you can use to find fellow-Asatruars in your local community or the area you live in.

The Asatru Folk Assembly is a global organization with branches and representatives found in many parts of the world. You can visit their website **https://www.runestone.org/** for more information. In addition to helping you in your research about Asatru and its customs and traditions, you can also go to their "Folkbuilder" page and connect with a team member. They, in turn, can help you find someone closer to where you live.

Another Asatru community with a presence on the Internet is The Troth **https://thetroth.org/**. You can register yourself there if you wish. Scout under the "Find your local troth representative," and you are likely to discover an individual or group closer to your place of residence.

Get in touch with the kindred in the cities closest to you and connect with them. Most of these people will have some idea of how to help you build your heathen connection. Here are a few tips to help you get started:

- Do an Internet search with the words "Asatru/kindred/Heathen, [your city name]" using different search engines. You are likely to get some results from such searches, including names, contact numbers, and addresses. You can begin with this basic information.

- Use social media platforms to find Asatru connections. Many kindred groups have a dedicated page on most of the popular social media platforms.

- You can set up a local meet group using one of the paid apps that connect with other believers. Although you might have to spend money, it could be worth your efforts. Still, you need to use this only if the earlier attempts don't work.

- Another way of contacting Heathens is to get in touch with other Pagan believers in your area, such as Wiccans. Considering that many Heathens start their Asatru journey from Wiccan beliefs, these connections are likely to help you get in touch with practicing Asatruars.

<u>**Temples**</u>

Manheim opened in Denmark in 2016 and was the first pagan temple in the country since the Middle Ages.

Other modern Pagan temples currently operating are the Ásaheimur Hof, in Efri Ás, Skagafjörður, and the Arctic Henge (Heimskautsgerðið), in Raufarhöfn in Iceland. The Odinist Fellowship Temple, in Newark-On-Trent in the United Kingdom, the Baldurshof, Asatru Folk Assembly temple, in Murdock, Minnesota, the New Grange Hall Ásatrú Hof, in Brownsville, Yuba County, California, and the Thorshof, Asatru Folk Assembly temple, in Linden, North Carolina, in the United States.

Apart from those, there are two temples under construction, one in the United States and one in Iceland.

The first is the Atlanta Heathen Hof, which will be a temple for the group Vör Fórn Siðr. It is 10 miles outside Atlanta, Georgia, and will hopefully be fully completed by 2022.

The second one is in Reykjavik, Iceland. The Hof Ásatrúarfélagsins is under construction by the Ásatrúarfélagið and is currently being built in stages as it has been delayed several times.

Here is a small list of kindred you can connect to, learn from, or contact to find your fellow Heathens. You can send them an email and ask for their contact details or pose your questions:

Northern Mist Kindred – Located in Oakland County in Southern Michigan, the Northern Mist Kindred is a large group of Pagans with followers from different branches of Paganism. This group is focused on improving their knowledge and wisdom about Paganism and its varied belief systems.

Kenaz Kindred – This group follows and worships the pantheon of Nordic gods and goddesses and focuses on the conservation of our planet and nature. They accept people from all cultural and racial backgrounds into their fold because they believe everyone has the right to worship and follow Norse Paganism and its gods and deities. They believe in the Nine Noble Virtues of the Odinic Rite. They are located in Eugene, Oregon.

Shieldwall Kindred – Based out of Utah, this small Asatru group's primary aim is to expand their membership, gain knowledge and wisdom, and share it with people who don't know about Heathenism and its authentic nature. This group believes strongly in the Aesir and Vanir gods, and they respect the influence these gods have on Midgard and its people.

People from all races and communities are welcomed into this group, and they do not restrict entry only to people of Germanic origin. According to their belief, their gods and goddesses traveled all over the world, and therefore, everyone should be allowed into the Asatru fold. This group is dedicated to helping new Heathens build their knowledge about Heathenism so that they can imbibe

Asatru values and principles into their lives and expand their mental, physical, and spiritual capabilities.

Northern Pines Heathen Kindred – Located in Northern Ontario, this Heathen kindred believes in self-preservation and self-sustenance. They honor and maintain a deep connection with their ancestors and the Asatru community. They believe in following the kindred honor code strictly along with the Nine Noble Virtues.

They follow and celebrate the traditional Asatru feasts and festivals, organizing rituals, ceremonies, and celebrations according to each festival. They believe in and follow the Asatru pantheon of gods, including Tyr, Odin, Freyr, Skadi, *etc.*

Hammerstone Kindred – This kindred group is a family-friendly group and organizes trips for members and their families to areas of interest. The members meet regularly to study and discuss Heathenry topics, including lore, mythological stories, related history, and more. The members hold numerous rituals and ceremonies to honor their gods and goddesses and share knowledge and wisdom.

Oath Keepers Kindred – This group was established by a group of high school friends in 2015 in Wisconsin, and they have small chapters all over the state.

Northern Rune Kindred – This Universalist Heathen kindred allows entry to all people regardless of caste, creed, race, gender, and any other distinction. The gods and goddesses of the Aesir and Vanir tribes are revered and worshipped. The members strive to live by the Nine Noble Virtues as they build their knowledge about Heathenism. They are based out of Herrin, Illinois.

Wyrd Ways Kindred – Based in South Jordan, Utah, this family-oriented kindred group welcomes all who seek permission to enter the fold and come with the noble intention of learning and expanding their knowledge.

Ulfr and Aesir Kindred – Based on a strict military discipline theme, this kindred believes that it is not for everyone. They practice a mixture of Asatru, combining some old ways with the new. The group is quite orthodox in its approach. Based in Missouri, this group allows entry to people of all races, creeds, genders, and communities, but you have to prove your worth over your birth.

Hrafn and Ulfr Kindred – This group has members who follow different Pagan beliefs. Some are novice Asatruars, while some others have been practicing Heathenism for many years. The members have found their way into this Heathenry kindred from Druidic paths, Witchcraft, and Native American belief systems. This kid-friendly kindred conducts blot ceremonies in open areas as often as possible. They are located in Topeka, Kansas.

Laeradr – This close-knit small community of Asatru is based out of a remote place in Norway. They are located on the island of

Bjarkoy, an ancient territory of the Vikings. This island was a prominent region during the Viking Age and the Middle Ages. This kindred practices an inclusive, open-minded form of Heathenry and believes in human beings' deep connection with land spirits, gods, and ancestors.

There are many more such kindred groups, especially in North America.

Ancestors and Spirits

Since the Norse believed that those who died could continue to live and exert more power, they worshipped their dead ancestors. This tradition has been adopted and continues today, albeit with many variations depending upon the culture that holds it. But central to the belief of the Norse was the view that if the ancestors were well pleased, they would come back to protect their home and their people.

In Norse literature, we see two types of ghosts: the **haugbui** and the **draugr**. These powerful supernatural beings would guard their former possessions and haunt their community.

The haugbui was relatively harmless unless his burial mound was disturbed and deeply attached to places that were comforting to them when they were alive. Some were buried with an open grave door so that their relatives could bring food offerings, as the dead were known to always be hungry. The draugr, on the other hand, was the more malevolent ghost who haunted their family if they died in bad circumstances or were not buried properly. Some stories say they would wreak havoc in the village by killing animals and destroying property.

Gods and Goddesses Today

The Norse deities that Asatruar worship have recently become better known. Movies, comics, and TV shows have adapted various interesting gods and goddesses into mainstream pop culture. Most people are aware of the thunder god Thor, the trickster god Loki, the all-father Odin, and even the Valkyries.

Odin is the supposed leader of the Aesir gods and was also worshipped as a god of war. However, his role wasn't limited to being the god of a single aspect. Odin has been associated with various fields; he was even considered the god of poets. The one-eyed god was also called Woden/Wotan/Wodan in various records which have been unearthed. Odin's importance can be understood by tracing the source of the word "Wednesday" as it is derived from "Woden's Day." The one-eyed Odin was considered a wise man, well-versed in magic and it is said he gained all his knowledge by hanging himself on the Yggdrasil tree for nine nights, giving up his eye in the process. Odin also married the goddess Freyja and fathered many children, including Thor.

Freyja, also known as Friggs or Frey, is the goddess of fertility and sexuality. For this reason, she was very popular among women in ancient times. Freyja was Odin's wife, and she was the one who escorted all the fallen heroes to Valhalla along with her Valkyries. She's considered the goddess of beauty and love due to her relationship with fertility and sex. The Asatru gods are all assigned multiple roles, and they aren't limited in scope. The same can be seen in the case of Freyja, who was also worshipped as a goddess of the household because one of her roles was to protect married women.

Thor is the single most well-known Norse god due to the various comics and movies in which he features. He's portrayed as the god of storms, which is why he was also worshipped by many in later eras when the Vikings' focus shifted to farming rather than war. Thor is depicted as an embodiment of masculine energy, and just like his mother Freyja, he is also associated with fertility. This is due to his ravenous sexual appetite and similar sexual escapades to the Greek god of thunder Zeus. Thor wields a war hammer, Mjölnir, and he was called by the other gods whenever a beast or a giant threatened the peace established by Aesir.

Another very popular god of the Norse pantheon was Loki. Despite being an Aesir, Loki was devious and was considered a trickster god. Contrary to the popular depictions of Loki, he's not the brother of Thor or adopted son of Odin. Loki is considered to be similar to

Odin in terms of stature and has also been depicted as Odin's brother in many places. He, along with the above-mentioned 3 major gods, was a major deity. It's even predicted that during Ragnarök—the Norse apocalypse, Loki would shift his allegiances and fight alongside the Jotnar to kill Odin. However, Loki wasn't an evil god by any means. He was a balancing power who questioned everything and expanded the boundaries of a society in which order was maintained by Odin and the others.

The way ancient heathens viewed their deities is largely different from the ways other polytheistic religions view their gods. This holds for the modern practice of Asatru as well. In the modern world beyond this riveting ancient religion, people like to categorize things into neat boxes, and the mere attempt to mix these things is often frowned upon. It is the reason people are still fighting to keep a binary gender identification or try to oppose the mixing of two races. Asatru religion is not like that, and it has always been quite progressive and beyond its time. The lines in this religion continue to blur, allowing space for more ideas, better definitions, clarifications, and analysis. The gods and goddesses in Asatru are rather humanistic and almost "real."

For example, Odin, who is generally known as a Norse God of War, is rarely associated with destruction or warfare in primary Asatru sources. Odin is so much more than a problematic war god that encourages bloodshed. He is associated with intelligence, wisdom, magic, poetry, and knowledge way before he is connected to war. When a modern heathen speaks of a deity, they do not assign an immortal value. They recognize that these deities have their own stories and that ancient heathens worshiped them for their unique characteristics. Being a polytheistic religion, there are so many deities that a person can connect to, depending on their personalities, desires, and characteristics. Once they spiritually connect with a heathen god or a goddess, they believe that they can communicate with them through dreams, intuitive messages, dreams, and such. Some believe that gods can directly affect the everyday happenings in their lives, and some believe that they have a broader spiritual purpose. Just like every other aspect of Asatru, it is all open to individual interpretation.

Asatru deities are not immortal, unlike many religions that worship gods. According to folklore, they perish in Ragnarok—the final destruction of the world in a conflict between deities. While some of the modern Asatru practitioners also believe in the form of Ragnarok, they consider it to be a metaphor for the many destructions in the world rather than a war of gods that would happen. According to source materials, some believe this war has already happened. They have chosen not to worship the old gods that are believed to have died during Ragnarok.

The all-knowing and omniscient god concept also does not exist in Asatru, which is another reason it tends to attract many modern practitioners who believe in the form of deities but do not believe that they are all-powerful and all-knowing. They make mistakes just as a human would, even Odin, who is known to have the most wisdom and knowledge. He gets tricked by his wife Frigga on occasion, according to folklore. This authentic nature of portraying gods is particularly appreciated and celebrated by modern heathens, prompting even the entertainment industry to create fictional characters inspired by Norse and Asatru folklore.

Incorporating Norse Magic into Daily Life

Just as the Germanic tribes incorporated Norse magic into their daily lives, we can do the same today. To the Old Norse, magic was knowledge, as large a part of their life as possessing agrarian skills or battle skills.

Norse magic has always been a way to understand our place in the world and a way to create the life we want to live through our will. Magic could guide our lives and help us control it. While this is important today, it was even more important during the Iron Age and the age of the Vikings. There was always much to question. Using magic rituals to uncover your fate, make plans to change that which was ordained by the Norns was crucial. Knowing what fate had planned, you could respond in an honorable way to any challenges or even devise ways to influence or affect your life's preordained plan.

With that in mind, Norse magic was then and is now a way to add a layer of control and understanding to your life. The Norse people did not view their fate as something that would prevent them from exercising their free will. They believed that we could aid and construct our will to best benefit the situations ahead. There was a certain sense of freedom in not having to guess our preordained future life. Within those constraints, we could achieve great things. Magic was a way to enhance their ability to do just that.

Today, the use of magic easily coincides with our desire to self-actualize, to accept where we are in life, and work to make our lives better. Magic was always a way to frame and respond to challenges, which were many in the time of the Vikings. Today, we have modern medicine and healthcare and the guidance of education. Yet, the appeal and strength of magic are still very strong. Norse magic was one of the earliest recorded ways humans attempted to better control their lives and understand that the world was more than just themselves.

Magic helped the people who practiced it to protect themselves against evil, successfully handle illness, and attempt to improve relationships, both personal ones and with the land itself. With the focus on survival being both successes in battle and an agrarian life and many farmsteads and family groups isolated from one another, it was through the practice of magic, the knowledge of skilled magic practitioners, and the faith in magic's healing properties that communities could unite.

Magic was not only the knowledge of the mystical and the natural worlds but it was also based on practical wisdom. The runic alphabet grew in use and from the desire to invoke magic. Magic led to literacy and understanding of the "other," which is located beyond the most provincial and small groups.

Fulltrúi and Ástvinr -Jotnar and Trolls and Wight

Asatru is an animistic faith. This is the belief that everything, including objects and places, possesses a certain spiritual essence. Animism believes almost everything, such as rivers, weather systems, and rocks contains a spirit or a wight. These spirits tend to be neutral towards humans; they can be pleased with offerings or angered with bad behavior.

The Wights go by many names, such as the Huldafolk in Iceland. The Isle of Wight in England is said to have etymological connections to the Wights.

Wights or Vaettir means land spirits, but there are also sea spirits and various other types. These different spirits of various nature-based origins symbolize the personal aspects and characteristics of nature. They represent the living, breathing attributes of nature.

Spirits and wights are often used interchangeably. Historically, the wights were considered to be as important as the Gods, sometimes even more so. This was because the wights, especially the land wights, are linked to the land they inhabit. The wight's guard protects and nourishes the land and those who dwell in it, as long as they are good spirits. As humans lived on and often lived off the land by growing food, much gratitude was directed at the wights. As the wights were so closely tied to the land, it was believed that they had a much bigger say in what goes on than the Gods do. Because of their responsibility, they looked after the land the best, and gratitude was to be directed their way. This is why many revered the wights more than the Gods.

Many would pray to the land wights, asking for rain or healthy crops. As if those who lived on the land needed it, the wights would too. It would serve more benefit to them, so the wights would often be the first port of call to offer prayers. Many make offerings to the wights; simple offerings could include a plate of food. A few players are read over the plate and left outside. This demonstrates to the wight, goodwill, and respect. The wights are, therefore, more likely to grant requests if offered a gesture of goodwill. Honoring the wights for their everyday roles on the land keeps them in good spirits and ensures they continue protecting the land.

A libation could also be offered; this is the same as an offering but in liquid form. Once prayers are read over the liquid, it is then poured into the earth. The energy of the liquid infused with the prayers reaches the wights who live on the land. This energy infuses them with respect and honor. As a continuous offering and kind gesture, respect is shown to the land. It is recommended to avoid destroying nature or disrespecting the land. If parts of nature need to be cut down, such as a tree, for a necessary purpose. An offering should be made first, and respect is shown to all elements of nature. By disrespecting the land, the wights could be angered, and this affects their protection of the land. The wights can turn against the land and those who dwell in it as a form of punishment.

When dealing with wights, politeness is of the utmost importance. Dissimilar to the demons of ceremonial magic, which are dominated and can be harshly commanded, wights have free will. Wights have no reason to wish humans ill or deny help. That is unless they feel personally offended.

Land wights are considered to be the guardian spirits of the woods, streams, and forests. They tend to be friendly but prefer not to be disturbed by modern man. They are known to befriend humans and even offer help in the form of helping crows to grow and other agricultural activities. They dislike blood and violence. The Land Wights have shapeshifting abilities and can appear in various forms.

They are their strongest in the wild, as this is where they thrive due to shying away from civilized spaces. Due to their shy nature, they have easily driven away from areas which can lead to these lands failing to prosper. Land Wights usually swell in areas such as springs or rocks.

Trolls

Some tales from Sweden describe trolls as monstrous beings with many heads who can either live in the forest and mountains or caves. The first kind of trolls that live in the mountains are known to be large, aggressive, stupid, and slow beings, always getting outwitted by the hero in the story. Those that live in caves are shy and seen as shorter than humans with stumpy arms and legs but with a fair amount of intelligence. They use the environment around them to influence their power or protect themselves and hide. These creatures emerged into mythology from the idea of the giants (jötun) in their cosmology and realms, as the word troll in Old Norse is *jätte*.

Giants

These supernatural beings of the natural world have, from the beginning of time, been the arch-rivals of the Æsir and Vanir. They often warred, fought, cheated, and married each other. The *jötun* live in the icy realm of Jötunheim, which is closely connected to Midgard by mountain ranges and dense forests, while the fire giants live in Múspellsheimr, their realm of fire. They are the catalyst of the great ending in Ragnarök, setting fire to the tree Yggdrasil and ending everything in flame.

What one would think of giants in physique is their immense stature, but in fact, they were no bigger than an average human and resembled the humanoid beings of other realms. They represented the original nature of chaos and destruction in comparison to the gods representing life and order.

Jotners

These are a race of giants which are separated into different categories, including frost and storm giants. It is said that Jotuns are a type of powerful creatures on the same level as Gods. Although considered giants, not all of them are big, and some are even the same size as humans. Many of the Jotuns are friendly with the Gods; however, some have friction with them. Despite this mix of friendliness and enmity, some of the Jotuns and the Gods inbreed. Uller's wife Skaoi and Freyr's wife, Gerd, are Jotuns. All of the Gods have a majority giant ancestry.

Today many view the Jotuns as the biggest of the land spirits. It is now believed the Jotuns need to be helped to restore the balance instead of being battled against. Some have stuck to the traditional viewpoint that giants are inherently destructive and peace should not be made with them.

Choose the Right Path for You

Among the multiple existing Pagan religions, you can choose any path that fits your purpose. You can become a Wiccan, a Hindu, an Agnostic Pagan, or follow any other faith you like. You just have to ensure that the religion you choose is suitable for your personality and future. The point of faith is to give direction to your daily life and provide peace to your psyche.

Answer these questions based on the core beliefs of Paganism to figure out a direction for your belief:

Do you feel close to nature and wish to protect it?

Do you believe in the cycle of birth, death, and rebirth?

Are you sensitive to the consequences of your actions?

Do you believe in individual moral and ethical freedom to attain peace?

Are you empathetic to the suffering of animate as well as inanimate beings?

Are you open to believing in multiple deities or one absolute God?

Have you always been fascinated by magic as a lifestyle?

Are you simply curious about the diverse faiths in existence?

Do you want to gain exposure to different cultural practices for research purposes?

If your answer to most of these questions is "yes," you agree with some fundamental beliefs of Paganism. If you are more inclined to the last two questions, you may want to become an expert or study Paganism academically. You will need to build a practical plan if you want to be a modern practitioner of Paganism.

The first step is to be specific. Avoid reading too many random sources on the internet without planning the path you want to follow. A good strategy is to research particular concepts like Wiccan rituals and Pagan traditions. Ask yourself what you are attracted to; Neo-Druidism, Shamanism, Asatru, or Green Witchcraft? Think deeply about what ideologies you have and how they match with each Pagan tradition. For example, if you care about environmental conservation and women's rights, the Neo-Wiccan or Green Witchcraft can offer you a chance to flourish. You might be an academic interested in learning about the different cultural impacts of Paganism; if that is your goal, begin streamlining your research.

A tip for researching is to find basic facts on religion and learn about its core beliefs. This will also help you in sieving through the myths and misconceptions attached to contemporary Paganism. You must make sure your decision is based on a realistic idea of what it means to be a Wiccan or Neo-Pagan. Additionally, you must research all the Pagan beliefs, history, specific religious movements, influences, and transformations over the centuries. This will help you to make a final decision on what enamors you. You can also choose to follow multiple outlooks.

Most Pagan faiths have a process of initiation. Find out how to become a part of a coven or a community and coach yourself on specifics. You may feel uncomfortable or overwhelmed if you are unaware of the sacrifices and actions you need to take up. For instance, if you want to be a Druid, you need to go through a structured initiation process. You cannot simply initiate yourself. There are levels of achievement and criteria that must be met for your successful membership; however, you can also choose to follow an individual path and become a solitary Pagan.

If you are still confused, read your sources closely. Pick up more books and do a close reading of each aspect. Ask yourself – does this make sense to you? Do you think it's ridiculous to believe in a certain aspect of the faith? Are you unclear about the topic? When you list out your fears and apprehensions, you will be able to engage in introspection better. Think about the author of the book – do you relate to them? Faith is deeply personal, and you need to make sure you relate to the community you want to join.

A great tip is to prepare a list of pros and cons. Take a piece of paper, divide it into two parts - on the left side, list pros, and use the right side to list cons. When you translate your conflicts on paper, you get a visual look into your thoughts. Having these ideas side by side will help you figure out the stakes involved in each benefit or potential harm.

You need to get a real picture of your desire to follow a certain path. You can go to the public library to read specific books. Thrift stores with second-hand books are also a good place to find specific books for study. The internet is another resource you can use to your advantage. Make sure the online resources you are referring to are legitimate and well-researched. Read book reviews and follow community threads to figure out which authors you like. Once you have built a library for yourself, you can refer to it for clarity whenever you wish. If you are still unsure about the reading list, check out study guides for beginners on sites dedicated to Paganism. It is impossible to read everything, and therefore, you should do a strategic reading. Some books might be metaphysical with tough terms and ideas. You need to spend time – develop a solid base for your intellectual concerns. Noting down arguments that interest you – whether you agree with them or not – is a method to compile your thought process in one place.

Such research will help you discover networks that will connect you to covens or groups. People who practice faith are the best resource for understanding the lifestyle of a Pagan. Finding folks with similar ideologies will help you discover a community of people and realize what you want for yourself. You can join a Meetup or go to local Spiritual stores and interact with people there. They can guide you to legitimate information. Even if you want to be a solitary practitioner, you can still approach people to brainstorm with them. Online chats and support groups can help you talk to real sorcerers and experienced magic practitioners.

How to Join a Norse Religious Group

The Norse Faith is full of rituals and customs, which, sadly, weren't written down until long after it stopped being the predominant faith of Scandinavia and Iceland. As already mentioned, the Old Norse faith had neither a strict hierarchy nor did they rely on rigid scriptures. Today's practice is no different.

The current practice of the Norse religion is about central ideologies such as the veneration of our ancestors and polytheism, without having strict rules on how to perform such practices. Although some congregations employ spiritual leadership, the common characteristic of the Norse faith is that it is relatively amorphous, non-authoritarian, and decentralized. However, it is not disorganized.

The Ásatrú method is the best example of getting formally inducted into a Norse Adherent group (which is usually commonly referred to as a hearth or the kindred). The method of Ásatrú is as follows:

In the presence of a goði or gyðja and the local goðorð, the newcomer pronounces their solidarity with and devotion to the Æsir and the Vanir. Then they affirm their allegiance to the Ásatrú way of living and renounce all other religions and faiths. These affirmations are usually done on a sacred object, like an oath ring.

The Norse adherents are not obligated to try to convert others or to spread the religion. They openly acknowledge that the Norse faith is not suitable for everyone or universal in any way.

A great way of getting in touch with the Asatru faith and finding your way within it is by connecting to other practitioners and heathens.

Having a mentor or welcoming community can help you learn more about the faith and add a certain nuance to some of the more abstract concepts and tenets of Asatru. It also gives you a sense of community and helps you transition to a heathenistic lifestyle.

Surrounding yourself with a supportive community also offers you companionship, which is quite important in the faith. It makes it easier to learn and grow within your faith.

Are there any general practices that you could follow to start with? Of course! Numerous practices within Asatru are implemented by practitioners, although the exact methods they employ are sure to differ.

A point that I feel is important to make is that, as a religion, Asatru isn't much for daily practices or conversing with the gods every day. How often you practice and how you practice is completely up to you.

Common practices include making offerings to the gods and goddesses and perhaps prayers, but they're less common.

That being said, certain practices and rituals are considered quite important. In its most basic form, Asatru involves celebrating a few major festivals each year. These festivals occur on the solstices, equinoxes, and cross-quarter day, although there are a few exceptions to this rule.

Now, when you think of festivals, it would be expected to imagine these large parties that stretch throughout a town and involve the entire community. The Asatru festivals are quite different, and while they are parties, they are often more intimate affairs and are generally held among families or Asatru groups.

Within Asatru, two major types of ritual celebrations are carried out to honor the Norse pantheon. The first is called the Blot and the second is the Sumbel. Also, numerous social and cultural events may vary from practitioner to practitioner.

Here are a few common ways to practice within Asatru:

The Blot and Sumbel

Blot is easily one of the most important practices within Asatru. Generally, when performing a Blot, a group or individual will gather in a secluded area and offer food and drink to the gods (Dees, n.d.).

There are numerous ways to perform the Blot, depending on how strictly the practitioners are focusing on the offering. Most Blot ceremonies involve a bowl of alcohol, generally mead, and this is taken as a sign that all present are partaking in the ceremony.

After, it is customary to seek blessings or favors from the gods, and the rest of the mead is offered to the earth. This is the final offering.

Blot can also be performed alone, which is great for individual practitioners. Think about a toast for a fallen soldier, pouring a drink into the fire or the ground. The same action can be performed for Blot.

Some practitioners might even choose to perform Blot daily or at every mealtime to thank the gods for their blessing and protection.

The Sumbel ritual is very similar to Blot and involves offering food or drink. The major difference is in the intent of the ritual.

Unlike Blot, Sumbel is a group ritual where the gods, heroes of old, and sometimes ancestors, are honored with offerings. It is also not so much a ritual performed for the gods, but rather it is a ritual performed in the presence of the gods.

Often, a drinking horn is passed around and shared among participants so that all can drink together. According to the traditions, oaths forged during Sumbel can never be broken.

Be Active in Your Community

Now, this practice is not as 'official' as Blot or Sumbel, but the practices within Asatru rarely are. The Blot and Sumbel are key parts of practicing Asatru; they are not the only ways.

As I've mentioned, for most practitioners, Asatru is a way of life and can be practiced in various ways.

There is a saying in Asatru that goes, 'we are our deeds.' For me, practicing Asatru forms part of every aspect of my life, and the things I do reflect my beliefs. My deeds and my beliefs cannot be separated. Nor can I separate myself, my experiences, or my perceptions from my family, my community, and my environment.

All of these aspects make me who I am. There is a great saying that goes, 'I am because you are,' which I think perfectly encapsulates what it means to truly be part of a community. Humans, by nature, are social creatures, and the concept of community is vital to our growth and development.

It is in my best interest and the interest of those around me to actively participate and improve the community; however, becoming an active member of your community can be hard.

I would suggest you start small. Try volunteering at a local shelter or organization such as an orphanage or homeless shelter. You could also volunteer your time to help at local schools.

The point is to try to give back to the community in any way that you can. Find something that you're passionate or interested in and get involved.

Care for Nature

While not necessarily a key tenet, Asatru does focus on the importance of nature and respecting the environment. Now, as with many aspects of Asatru, this aspect is up for interpretation.

What does respecting the environment mean to you?

For some, this could mean starting a community garden or volunteering at an organization focused on conservation and nature. It could mean starting a private garden or caring for plants.

I'll be the first to say that I don't have a green thumb, nor am I particularly interested in plants or gardening. Therefore, when I practice, I focus on the preservation of nature. For example, cleaning up a park or beach.

Caring for nature can also be interpreted as caring for wildlife and animals. You could volunteer or work with animals.

My point is that we can honor the gods in numerous ways, and not all of them involve participating in rituals or ceremonies.

Be Careful with Your Words

Within Asatru, words hold power. They matter. The words you speak not only affect you but also the people around you. It is believed that the words you speak also affect your wyrd (your fate or destiny) as well as the wyrd of those around you.

Therefore, words hold immense weight and shouldn't be used carelessly.

The importance of this can be seen in the weight placed on oaths and vows. To break a vow or oath is to dishonor yourself.

Therefore, a good way to practice Asatru is to be careful with your words. Try to be as truthful as you can, don't make promises you can't keep, and don't use your words to hurt others.

How you choose to interpret these suggestions will depend on your morals and values.

Pray

Norse Pagans don't pray conventionally, and there's no specific way to follow when it comes to praying.

Some prefer to hold group gatherings and make offerings to the gods, while others prefer to do the same on their own, in private.

Others plan and perform elaborate rituals, while some prefer just to talk.

Some might even borrow methods and rituals from other faiths and practices.

As the Faith is decentralized, not everyone agrees on which is the right way, but most agree that the gods are like family to them.

Most Norse adherents prefer not to pray with their gods in a conversational tone. This usually occurs outdoors, just like the Old Norse pagans used to. There are specific sites, like the Danish Hof Manheim, meant for rituals and ceremonies.

Perform Rituals

Many of the rituals that modern Norse pagans perform are the same as the ones Vikings and other Old Norse people performed. Some of these rituals involve:

Honoring the gods

Giving offerings

Feasting together

Raising a toast to one of the Gods

Praying to the Gods

The main way of praying to the Norse gods is by focusing our thoughts on the deity we wish to invoke or by chanting prayers around a bonfire with other members of our hearth.

Sacrifices and offerings can be made through the blot on traditional holy days. People can also honor the Gods through their actions and words during the Sumble or a daily ritual.

In the Old Norse religion, most of the festivals were interwoven with village and farm life aspects. Survival was the ultimate goal; so, a lot of the blot or blood sacrifices were performed according to the phases of the moon to ask for a good and fruitful harvest.

The most common sacrifices in ancient times were animal sacrifices, but human sacrifices also occurred. The latter, though, was reserved for extreme conditions, such as war or famine. During those times, prisoners were offered to the Gods.

Artifacts were also often offered, as there has been archaeological evidence in fens and bogs, such as jewelry, weapons, and tools. This method is the preferred manifestation of offering in modern Norse Pagan rituals. One thing to make sure of is that none of the objects offered would harm or pollute nature.

The Old Norse used to offer mead to the Æsir. However, as mead is not very common nowadays, most modern pagans prefer to give offerings of beer or wine. Offerings aren't meant to placate the gods but to express the adherent's devotion to them.

According to the lore, Óðinn loves poetry. A good way to get Óðinn's attention is to do it in the form of a poem. All in all, the Norse's way of praying is not at all similar to what one might have in mind.

Asatru Runes and Charms as Practiced Today

Esoteric arts are a system of arts, charms, and magical culture that is connected to Asatru religion and heathenry. Many runes, incantations, charms, bands, and other magical tools are used in this particular art, and while it has faded away to some extent over the years, they are widely used even today. Runes include an advanced and magical alphabet when employed in carvings and paintings related to Asatru rituals. Divination or predicting the future is a common way modern Asatru practitioners use runes. Runic divination involves reading omens and deciphering natural signs to predict a certain good or bad outcome that may happen in the future. It also requires a lot of intuition and other magical rituals connected to the religion, such as spell work and herb magic.

Runes and Charms that come from the Asatru religion have inspired many modern spiritual practices and literature. The origin of these practices goes back centuries ago. There are stories of merchants who sailed the seas having stone tags with protective rune carvings and young lovers using runes and charms to attract their beloved. When studying folklore, the father of runes is considered to be the intelligent leader Odin, who is known for sending omens and similar signs to communicate with his followers. It is said that when Odin was learning ancient runes, the power was so great that they brought him to tears. Large volumes of ancient documents are written in runes with origins in Scandinavia, Iceland, and Germany that modern heathen continue to study and get inspiration from.

To speak of one of the most common ways runes are used in the modern era, the throwing or casting method is quite popular among the modern heathens. They keep their runes in a bag or a container. Whenever there is an issue or a situation they need a complex answer to, they focus on that issue and grab a rune from the container without looking. Then they cast or throw a handful of runes to a cloth or the altar. Then they examine the pattern in which the runes were fallen on the cloth or the stone slab and read the pattern to give themselves an idea about their situation.

Asatru is a universal and timeless religion being practiced after many centuries, relating to people authentically and spiritually. Something extremely pure and nostalgic about this ancestral religion makes it captivating to people after many years. It speaks to the purest parts of a person's heart; it is closer to nature. It allows plenty of space for analysis and interpretation, which is refreshing in a theistic religion and does not have the restrictive dogma be seen in many mainstream religions. Therefore, it is likely that people will practice Asatru many years after as a diverse, inclusive, and unrestrained religion.

The Three Nornir: Urðr, Verðandi, and Skuld

A poem in the *Poetic Edda* called "Fjolsvinnsmal" refers to the Tree of Life as Mimir's Tree or Mimameid. It is also known as Lerad, a tree so huge that its twigs and leaves provide food for the goat, Heidrun, and the stag, Eikþyrnir, that live on the roof of Valhalla.

Three roots support the Yggdrasil. One of these roots passes through Asgard. The second one passes through Jotunheim, and the third one goes through Helheim. The sacred Well of Wyrd where the three Norns or Nornir (the three Fates) lived was beneath Asgard's roots. Even the gods had no control over the Well of Wyrd.

The Well of Mimir (or Memory), Mimisbrunnr, lay beneath the root of Jotunheim while the well Hvergelmir (or the Roaring Cauldron) lay beneath the Helheim root.

The World Tree is an essential element to the story of Ragnarok. According to prophecies in Norse mythology, only two human beings would survive the Ragnarok, namely Lif and Lifthrasir. These two people would escape from the brunt of the war by sheltering themselves in Yggdrasil's branches and consuming the dew on the World Tree leaves.

Fate and Luck In the ancient stories, we learn that the world and humans are fated. Some of the stories feature the ***nornir***, the female spirits of fate, and while nobody knows exactly how many there are, three of them are mentioned by Snorri Sturluson and in the Eddic poem ***Vøluspá*** (The ***Vølva***'s Prophecy): Urðr, Verðandi, and Skuld. The nornir live by the well called Urðarbrunnr at the foot of Yggdrasill, the tree that stands in the middle of the world and represents the cosmos. An eagle sits in its crown and a serpent lies among its roots; time flows like water through the tree, and from the crown falls the dew and rain, which flows over the world's soil and collects in the well. These three ***nornir*** control the fate of humans and the world. The three nornir, Urðr, Verðandi, and Skuld, represent the past, present, and future. They weave threads of fate for humans, tie them in the tree, and cut them when it is time. Skuld cuts rune-sticks for each human to set their fate and lifespan.

Every Ásatrú group and family has unique birth rituals. There is not a uniform ancient custom to refer to in modern times. However, an ancient tradition is the **nornagraut**, the **norns'** porridge. The goddesses of fate called the **nornir** are responsible for setting the fate of a human with fate-threads when they are born. This is beautifully described in the heroic Eddic poem **Helgaqviða hundingsbana in fyrri**, in stanza 3: **"Snero þær af afli ørlögþátto, þá er borgir braut í Brálundi; þær um greiddo gullin símo oc und mána sal miðian festo."**

("They [the **nornir**] turned powerfully the strings of fate when burrows shook in Brálund [on Earth]; they tangled the golden threads and set them in the middle of the Moon's Hall [the sky].") To give the **nornir** thanks for setting a good fate for the newborn, it was an old custom (in the Faroe Islands, Denmark, and Setesdal in Norway) for the woman who had given birth to share **nornagraut** with the **nornir**. People would prepare a special porridge and the woman would share it with her married female friends, including a portion that was given to the **nornir**. The tradition also existed among the Sámi, who would prepare Sárakka-porridge for the goddess Sárakka. Both in the Sámi tradition and the Danish tradition, people would place three sticks in the porridge. In the Sámi tradition, one stick would be white, one would be black, and the third one would have three rings carved on it. The sticks would be put under the threshold of the door before nightfall, and they would tell the fortune of the mother and child based on which of the sticks had been taken during the night. There is no similar information about the Danish custom with the sticks, except that they seem to have represented the three **nornir**: Urðr, Verðandi, and Skuld.

In the Faroese and Danish traditions, there is also the idea of **nornaspor**. If a child has a white spot on its nail, it is a **nornaspor** (**norn**'s mark), and it tells the fortune of the child. This has a counterpart in the Eddic poem **Sigrdrífomál**, where stanza 7 says that power-runes should be carved on the drinking horn, the back of your hand, and—to gain power-runes—you should mark your nail with **nauð**, the n-rune: n. The n-rune has been used in magic formulas since the earliest times. In an old Anglo-Saxon charm for healing, from the 11_th_ century, it says, **"Neogone wæran Noþðæs sweoster"** ("They were nine, Nauð's sisters"). This seems to be another reference to **nornir**—here including the magical number nine, too. It is clear that the **nornir** were considered healing powers and traditionally were believed to have a hand in birth.

The Main Actions to Follow to Profess the Norse Religion

If you wish to practice Ásatrú, this is my advice to you:

• Get a good copy of the Poetic Edda and the Prose Edda.

• Get a good copy of a compilation of the Sagas of Icelanders.

• Begin experimenting with the way that you would like to connect with the gods and spirits yourself before you seek out a group. Groups can be very rewarding, but it is important to create your independent foundation for how you relate to your gods before you open up to outside influence.

• The best groups are always those based on friendship more than anything else. Real and honest friendships drive a good group of heathens much further than hierarchies and ideas of true faith.

• Always follow Óðinn's advice in the Hávamál. It will be hard to go wrong when you keep that advice in mind. They are the cumulation of hard-earned lessons through countless years, decades, and centuries.

• Always follow your heart. It is that simple.

Chapter 7: What is Asatru

Understanding Asatru

Asatru is a modern religion based on pre-Christian Germanic views. Asatru builds on the surviving records of their past belief system, and the followers have worked hard to keep as close as possible to the religion of the original Norse people.

Asatru loosely means "belief in the sir," which likely means the gods. Broken down, Asatra is made of "asa" which is the possessive of 'sir, meaning Aesir, and "tru" which is religion or belief.

In 1972 Asatru became recognized as a legitimate religion thanks to the poet Godi Sveinbjorn Beinteinsson. Since then, the religion has started to grow rapidly among former Norse countries, North America, and Europe.

It's common for many religions to become corrupted with homophobic, sexist, racist, and antisemitic beliefs. Fortunately for Asatru, since its resurgence, it has not been subject to any such corruption. In fact, they are strongly against racism and many other corruptions. Many groups even have these rules written into their constitutions. This applies to most English-speaking countries as well. However, some anti-racism groups have mistakenly called Asatru a racist religion.

Here's how the Asatru belief system works:

They are polytheistic. They believe that three main races of Deities live among us and are involved in human life. These are the Aesir, Vanir, and Jotnar. They also worship the same gods and goddesses that we have already talked about. The most common are Thor, Odin, Freyr, Freya, Frigg, Skadi, and Ostara. They also honor the land spirits known as Landvaettir.

The North American Asatruars have come up with a list of the Nine Noble Virtues: perseverance, self-reliance, industriousness, hospitality, discipline, fidelity, honor, truth, and courage. They place great importance on the family and also reject all forms of discrimination based on sexual orientation, race, nationality, language, gender, or ethnicity, as well as any "other divisive criteria."

Their origin story follows the same origin story that the Old Norse people believed. Everybody is descended from Gods and Odin, Vili, and Ve made the first people: Ask and Embla. Rig, another deity, came along and created the different social classes.

They believe in a gift of ecstasy, called od, given to them by the Gods. This is what they consider to separate the humans from the other animals and is the eternal link to all the Gods.

Unlike the mainstream religions that believe a person goes to heaven or hell once they die based on how they lived their life, the Asatruar believe in several afterlife locations. The heroic individuals and warriors go to Folkvangr, Freyja's field. This is where everybody wants to go. Then you have Helheim, which is the neutral realm that most people end up in. Dishonorable people or oath breakers are consumed by Niddhog. Then the ones that die at sea are said to go to a different afterlife. However, many followers don't actually take the Norse myths literally. Many believe that they will be reincarnated along their family line. Others believe that the dead only inhabits their graves.

Of course, they believe that the end of the world will be Ragnarok, as explained above. At the end of the great battle, one man and woman will remain to repopulate the world and to live the same cycle over again

Though Asatru is an ancient practice, it was near extinct after Christianization hit Europe. Many were forced to follow a different religion and the ancient ways nearly disappeared.

However, they made a comeback in the 1970s as the revival of Germanic Paganism was celebrated once more. In Iceland, on the

Summer Solstice of 1972, it was recognized as an official religion once again. Shortly after, Asatru groups formed in the United States.

The religion is similar to the ancient ways of Norse culture, before Christianity.

Asatru is "true to the Aesir." Asatruars believe that gods are living beings who take an active role in the world. Much of the Asatru beliefs are based on Old Norse mythology. There are three types of deities within Asatru: the Aesir, the Vanir, and the Jotnar. The Aesir is the primary focus of worship of the deities, though worshipping the other two branches is also accepted. Some of the gods and goddesses include:

Odin, the one-eyed father figure who learned secret wisdom by hanging from Yggdrasil for nine nights.

Frigg, the wife of Odin, and goddess of marriage and motherhood with a talent for divinity and 'seeing.'

Freyr and Freya, the brother and sister deities of fertility, love, and battle.

Thor, Odin's son and the god of thunder who wields a divine hammer.

Loki, the trickster god who has, on numerous occasions, shown a lack of honor.

These gods were just a few among the many gods of the Aesir. Asatru followers may also worship several gods among the Vanir and Jotnar, though the focus should be primarily on Aesir gods.

Asatru also believes in the Nine Noble Virtues, Norse Paganism's version of the ten commandments. As with many things in Norse mythology, the sacred number nine appears. These virtues are the basic Norse standards of courage, honor, discipline, industriousness, hospitality, self-reliance, perseverance, truth, and fidelity.

Why Asatru Was Started

The Norse Pagan revival, like any other movement, was motivated by a variety of factors. After being an integral part of the culture of the Norse people for over ten centuries, it was slowly replaced by Christianity, leaving a gaping hole. The Norse people felt a distinct disconnect from their own culture. Over the years, Norse Paganism was completely stripped of its spiritual side, leaving only the myths remaining. Many modern people, feeling a severe disconnect from their culture of origin, turned to their past for an explanation, and this is where they discovered Norse Paganism.

Many others turned to Asatru for guidance because it aligned with their beliefs and their worldview or because it brought them the spiritual satisfaction they had been searching for. Last but not least, while not officially part of the Norse Paganist community, some of the first heathen groups used religion to amplify their right-wing political and ethnicist ideologies. While Asatru sought to strengthen connections between the Norse, their ancestors, and their cultures, it also sought to foster connections between the Norse and the rest of the world.

Norse Paganism never had a single governing entity, but it was and continues to be a highly decentralized religion with many organizations driven by their interpretations and understandings. The first movements emerged in the late 1960s and early 1970s. In 1969, Else Christensen, a Danish native, founded the Odinist Fellowship in the United States, which was regarded as the first instance of a racialist Paganist group in the U.S. Stephen McNallen, who established the Viking Brotherhood a few years later and ended up disbanding it due to constant clashes with neo-Nazis within the Brotherhood, is another founder. Then, in 1976, he founded the Asatru Free Assembly, which was more selective in terms of followers.

In 1972, the Ásatrúarfélagið organization was founded in Iceland where the main focus was to connect with the ancient culture and return to when the Icelandic were more connected to nature. As time passed, people started seeing the core values of Norse Paganism and steering away from political groups with ethnicist/racialist roots. By the 1990s and 2000s, most Asatruars had become privy to the differences between the devoted and the misguided.

In Iceland, Asatru was not recognized as a legal religion until 1973. It all started with the founding of Ásatrúarfélagið in 1972 by a farmer and a poet named Sveinbjörn Beinteinsson. After the organization was founded and attracted a small number of followers, Sveinbjörn went to the minister of justice and ecclesiastical affairs, Ólafur Jóhannesson, in December of 1972. The minister, as expected, refused and terminated the meeting. Now, there are two possibilities as to why he changed his mind. Later that day, a thunderstorm hit, cutting off electricity to the town's center where the minister worked. He may have perceived that as a sign. When asked, minister Jóhannesson stated that the Icelandic constitution guarantees the freedom to create any religious organization.

At the time, the Bishop of Iceland had a contradicting opinion. He stated that the constitution granted people the freedom to practice monotheistic religions rather than the freedom to practice polytheism. In response to his objections and his belief that the ideologies taught in Asatru were heavily linked to Nazism, the founder of Ásatrúarfélagið stated that most National Socialists were, in fact, Christians with no connection to the Asatru belief. In May of 1973, Ásatrúarfélagið was recognized as an official religious organization which meant they had the right to officiate weddings and conduct funerals, as well as public blots.

The first outdoor blot - since the ritual was banned by Christians in ancient times - took place in August of the same year. Since then, the organization has grown to the point where its members can carry out their plans to build temples and burial grounds. In terms of politics, Ásatrúarfélagið has been and continues to be a politically inactive organization.

Key Beliefs in Asatru

As mentioned previously, Asatru is a polytheistic faith and revolves around a pantheon of deities. It is believed that these deities take an active role in the world we live in and its inhabitants.

The Asatru believe in three sects of deities:

The Aesir: these deities form part of the main pantheon and represent leadership.

The Vanir: while not directly part of the pantheon, they are associated with it and represent nature and earth.

The Jotnar: these are giants that are often in conflict with the Aesir and are representative of destruction and chaos.

It is important to note here that most Asatru practitioners honor the Aesir over the Vanir and Jotnar.

Now, depending on your own set of beliefs and how you choose to practice Asatru, you could view the gods as metaphorical constructs that have emerged as a means to interpret the world, or you could view them as distinct beings with an active role in how the world is shaped.

Asatru, first and foremost, is a world-accepting religion. While it does acknowledge an afterlife, the focus is placed on living a good life on earth rather than living with the expectation that you'll enjoy an afterlife. The point is to live for the world you're in and not for a world, you cannot imagine.

The saying 'we are our deeds' perfectly encompasses this belief and states that the sum of our actions is what is truly important.

Another key belief is a sacrifice to the gods. This often occurs via sacred rituals and is performed as desired by the practitioner and community. There is no set rule; however, it does form part of the core celebrations of religious holidays like Yule and Midsummer.

The Mythology of Asatru

The Norse myths and tales the Asatru revolve around first emerged during the initial practice of heathenry. These myths and tales were told and acted as a representation of how people understood and perceived the world (Seigfried, 2021).

Often, these myths would also express their worldview and act as an explanation for their rituals and practices. Some Norse myths were intrinsically tied to the culture of practitioners. A key example of this is the myth of Thor, who shrunk his hammer to wear it around his neck. This myth influenced culture, and many practitioners wore miniature amulets of Thor's hammer around their necks (Seigfried, 2021).

In addition to the myth, what else did Thor's hammer symbolize? Was it strength? Protection? And what was the importance of wearing the hammer? Was it in honor of Thor?

These are the kinds of questions you should ask yourself when delving into the Asatru myths.

My point here is that myths are more than just stories passed on through generations. Myths are vital to the faith of Asatru, and the challenge modern practitioners face is taking these age-old myths and using them to try and find meaning in modern-day life. It is a challenge to root our modern practices in ancient myths, however, without those roots, our practices lose all meaning.

The Nine Noble Virtues

The Virtues are identical in both ancient and modern Norse Paganism. However, their application has evolved as a result of how much people's lives have changed. People used to live in tribes and villages, often having to prepare for disasters such as famines, harsh weather, and foreign attacks. Their primary needs were survival and physical safety, rather than emotional fulfillment or self-actualization and satisfaction. The values of courage, truth, honor, fidelity, discipline, hospitality, self-reliance, industriousness, and perseverance were established and practiced to ensure the tribe's unity and survival by holding each individual to a standard. They found strength and inspiration in the values which enabled them to live better, safer, and more stable lives.

We've evolved beyond the need to survive as the world has progressed, and we've put a significant distance between ourselves and famine and pillaging. Instead of needing a tribe or wealth for survival, we now want a tribe and wealth for added fulfillment or satisfaction. In modern times, the Noble Virtues are applied mindfully to fit the context of one's life, rather than strictly and thoughtlessly. Courage entails bravery in personal pursuits, in the workplace, and the face of hate speakers. Honor means living a life congruent with ourselves, a life that honors and celebrates ourselves and our needs and desires. Not only that but a life that respects the existence of other humans. As you can see, now that the need for safety has been met, the Virtues are there to guide followers along their journey of personal growth.

The Nine Noble Virtues (NNV) of Asatru and Norse paganism are a series of moral and ethical guidelines that stem from numerous historical and literary sources and myths.

Ancient Norse pagans held these virtues to be spiritual law and thus not up for debate. The ancient tribal laws stemmed from these virtues and began as customs and traditions. In those years, it was believed that we should first be well-versed in the spiritual laws and customs before approaching the Norse pantheon.

In modern times, following the NNV is hardly as strict, and Asatru offers its practitioners the freedom of practicing as they wish.

Here are the Nine Noble Virtues of Asatru:

Fidelity

Fidelity is the willingness to be loyal to your faith and belief systems, including the deities, and your community, friends, and yourself. There are many levels of loyalty, which are individual-specific and situational-specific. Each of us knows and understands the depth of the various levels of loyalty we feel within ourselves.

Fidelity in Asatru includes your commitment:

To your faith (Asatru).

To your community and kindred.

To your family responsibilities.

To your intention of making the world a better place.

Courage forms the foundation on which loyalty and commitment build their strengths. When we are courageous, we find the power to hold the bonds that tie us to our faith, community, and family. These bonds of togetherness drive us to accept ourselves as a conduit through which progress for the family and community takes place. These bonds of commitment are what weave the tapestry of Asatru.

Interestingly, "troth" is the German word for loyalty and faith. In ancient times, a warrior who survived while his lord died—or failed to die for his tribe or community's safety and protection—was dishonored and shunned by his society.

Fidelity is also about honoring your promises and oaths, including wedding vows. Oaths and promises are sacred contracts, and those who break these contracts are the biggest offenders, according to Asatru NNV.

Generosity and fidelity are connected at a very deep level. Giving is a way to strengthen fidelity. When you are loyal, then you find your ability to be generous and giving also improves. Giving is not only in the form of materialistic things but also in the gift of love, time, *etc.* Importantly, the act of generosity is not one-sided but has to work both ways. According to ancient Heathens, if you do not return the giver with your generosity, then you will lose the power of the gift you received.

A passage in Havamal on fidelity goes like this, "If you have a friend you trust, then you must pray for his goodwill, to exchange gifts and thoughts, and visit his house even as you invite him to your house as often as possible."

Perseverance

Perseverance is another virtue closely tied to courage. Within the context of the Nine Noble Virtues, perseverance means pushing forward and remaining steadfast despite the difficulty or number of obstacles in front of you.

It also means rising from our defeats and failures and learning from our mistakes and poor choices. The point here seems to be that by persevering, we will be able to live up to our fullest potential.

Persevering means having the courage to continue moving forward even when things get hard and frustrating.

The virtue of perseverance was especially important during ancient times when only those who were strong, clever, and innovative survived. The ancient Norse heathens didn't live in the relative comfort that we do, with our modern comforts of water heaters, stove tops, and shopping markets. Life was hard, and survival was not guaranteed.

Those times favored the people who persevered and learned to make the best of their circumstances. While we have developed a plethora of comforts in modern times, life still throws its hurdles at us.

The true test of a person is how well they persevere during adversity.

Courage

The Asatru defines courage as an element of pagan virtue that drives an individual to act and behave in the right way, even in the absence of reward or in the face of certain defeat. This definition emerged in all the Norse stories and legends. The powerful monsters are central to all Norse mythological themes, but they were not given an honorable character.

Contrarily, the heroes found potent solutions to kill the monsters driven by sheer courage and willpower. The concept of courage being paramount in a person's life is the reason, however misplaced, that gave rise to the opinions that the Vikings were godless.

The Viking people were so focused on their courage to do the right thing that they believed that martial heroism was a power of its own. In today's world, courage is more than martial bravery. It also means to stand up for the right thing. For example, turning into a whistleblower when the company you work for has violated laws is considered to be a courageous thing to do, according to the Asatru.

Norse Paganism believed that courage was all about having faith and trust in your strength. Courage, according to Asatru, also includes being brave to live according to the Nine Noble Virtues. Asatruars believe that it is vital to stand up in a hostile world to be counted among the authentic people of character.

Courage is:

Having the conviction and inner strength to face the enormity of the task at hand.

Standing by your friends and family.

Keeping alive and following Asatru principles.

Industriousness

The Nine Noble Virtues go a bit further and view industriousness as striving for efficiency and finding joy in the work itself instead of focusing solely on the outcome. Much like self-discipline and perseverance, industriousness views hard work and striving for improvement in all areas of life as a way to strengthen not only ourselves but our communities.

In ancient times, industriousness and hard work were vital for survival. If you didn't work hard, your chances of survival were low.

Unlike now, there weren't any grocery stores, and people grew or hunted for their food. Every aspect of life required work.

The sentiment that hard work means survival has carried on through the ages and is very relevant in modern society. After all, the harsh truth is that many of us need to work to survive.

We need to secure a stable job and earn an income to thrive in our modern-day capitalistic society. We don't have much choice.

For me, industriousness means more than just working hard and enjoying what you do. I interpret industriousness as not only being hard-working but also being innovative and finding new ways to improve your life and well-being.

Self-Discipline

The virtue of self-discipline is closely tied to the virtue of perseverance. According to the Nine Noble Virtues, self-discipline is the willingness to uphold your honor and the other virtues within the NNV.

After all, these days it isn't easy to stick to one's moral code, especially if you're surrounded by people who do not share your morals and values. Remaining steadfast in your beliefs and upholding your morals and values are key aspects of self-discipline.

By working hard, practicing self-discipline, and working on improving yourself is considered a manner of honoring yourself.

This is one of my favorite parts of Asatru. As you might have noticed, a recurring theme in the Nine Noble Virtues is practicing self-care and the promotion of reaching your potential. As much as the faith centers around the gods and ancestors, it also centers around the practitioner, and by caring for yourself, you are also honoring the gods.

Truth

Courage and truth are interlinked because courage fosters and encourages truth, and the reverse is also true. When you build your ability to speak the truth in your life, you also build the courage to face the consequences. Truth is the underlying virtue of holiness, even as it strengthens us toward being courageous. In the absence of truthfulness in your character, you are unlikely to meet with any kind of spiritual realization.

Being courageous and truthful requires persistent efforts. You must incessantly strive to do the right thing and live according to what you know and believe as being true and correct. Truthfulness is a virtue valued by our ancestors. Being truthful also helps you in being modest. You find it easy not to exaggerate your achievements as well as accept your failures with humility.

There is an interesting warning concerning speaking the truth. Undoubtedly, you must always try to speak the truth, but you must not be naïve enough to talk the truth with people who spout lies to you. According to the Havamal, it might be a good thing to counter lies with lies to guarantee that you are not taken for a ride by the scamsters of the world.

One of the verses about truth explained in Havamal goes as follows, "Do not promise something you cannot live up to. Breaking your word has serious consequences."

Honor

Honor is all about the value of recognizing and accepting nobility, both within and outside of us. Honor is not only your feeling of self-worth rooted in your noble character but also showing respect to others. Perhaps honor is one of the most difficult virtues to define because different people can interpret it differently.

The importance of living an honorable life is contained in this small proverb in the *Poetic Edda,* "Everything and everyone in this world dies. However, the reputation of dead people never dies." So, good or bad deeds survive even after our deaths, and they carry the glory or burden of our soul.

Hospitality

When guests come to your house, you must make them as comfortable as you can and offer them food and drink. Hospitality is a very important virtue in Asatru: their gods travel all over the cosmos, including to Midgard or the realm of human beings. With that in mind, a guest in your house could be a god in disguise, and you must honor him or her.

Also, hospitality drives a sense of readiness to help and assist people in need. It drives interdependence in the community and forges strong bonds among the members. In fact, for ancestors, hospitality was not just a virtue, it was a necessity. In those days, traveling long distances posed a lot of difficulties and was also dangerous. Yet, traveling was important for trade and commerce. Norsemen and women of those times freely opened their homes not only to their friends and other known tribespeople but also to strangers.

People who came knocking would be provided with a warm place to rest their tired feet, warm food to fill their bellies, and even warm clothes to wear. In return, the guest was expected to eat moderately, entertain their hosts with songs and stories, and give little gifts such as small trinkets. Havamal talks about the importance of hospitality in the following way: "A guest who has traveled needs the warmth of a fire for his numb knees, warm water to wash, clean clothes and food to fend off the hunger and cold."

Self-Reliance

This virtue reflects your spirit of independence. When you are self-reliant, you are independent for yourself and empower your family toward this virtue. It is important to remember that being self-reliant does not mean you should deny your interconnectedness with others. It is about having the ability to first take care of yourself and then work toward helping others in need. Self-reliance helps you provide food to eat for yourself and share what you have with others in need.

Self-reliance teaches you to find solutions for your problems. It teaches you to build skills to make your life better than it is today. It teaches you not to waste time and use your skills effectively to learn new things to bring prosperity to your life.

Self-reliance is a vital element of freedom. When you are self-reliant, you are free to make your own decisions. You can think for yourself and find solutions that suit you best. When you taste freedom, you earn more freedom, and you become increasingly self-reliant. Self-reliance is about using your wisdom and intellect to understand yourself and the world around you.

Asatru Perspectives

The modern Asatru/Heathenism community has three primary perspectives, namely, Universalism, Folkism, and Tribalism. Of these three, the first two perspectives are the main ones, while the third, Tribalism, takes a middle-ground approach.

Universalism – According to the people who believe in this perspective, anyone from any background can become a Heathen. A Universalist perspective offers more freedom of choice to everyone, even while giving greater options for Heathenism to grow and expand its reach across the globe.

Therefore, a Universalist will welcome a Japanese person into his or her fold of Asatru as long as the initiate is willing to understand the lore of Norse Paganism, live his or her life based on the nine virtues, learn and understand the runes of Asatru, and take responsibility for his or her actions. Most importantly, a Universalist values common sense.

One of the primary arguments against Universalism, especially from the Tribalists and Folkish, is that it is very open-ended. People of the other two perspectives believe that there should be a few vital threshold criteria that need to be met before allowing anyone to practice Asatru. Conversely, Universalists believe that these vital criteria are already there, those which have been discussed in the previous paragraph.

Folkism – The Folkish perspective believes that Asatru is an ethnic religion and entry should be restricted only to those with a North European heritage. This belief of Folkism is based on the idea that ethnic religions connect followers to the local landscape, bloodline, ancestors, and traditions. So, outsiders can't find a connection with the ethnic elements and will fail to be genuine practitioners.

Many people accuse those who follow Folkism of being white supremacists because of their rigid approach regarding their entry into Asatru, but the Folkish argue that their stand has nothing to do with white supremacy but is based on the deep belief that every ethnic community must worship its ancestors.

People who oppose Folkism also use another argument in their favor. They quote the presence of multiple non-Norse people and characters in the Eddas and other Norse folklore and legends. These non-Norse characters took part in rituals and rites too. Also, slaves in the Nordic community came from other lands and regions, including Slavic, Celtic, and even Middle Eastern. Many of these slaves were freed and emancipated by their masters and allowed to settle and live the Nordic life.

On the other hand, the Norse people who migrated to other lands also adopted and absorbed those lands' cultures and traditions. Despite these arguments, Folkism stands firm in its principle to not allow all and sundry into the Asatru fold.

Tribalism – Folkism and Universalism are at the two ends of the Asatru spectrum, while those who follow Tribalism take a middle stand. They accept and embrace the Folkish stand of the need for a deep connection and feeling for Norse culture to be able to call oneself an Asatru. Surface-level adoption of Asatru principles is not enough. A person can be inducted into the clan in one of two ways, specifically if he or she is of Germanic origin or if the person is converted, adopted, or takes an oath into the community.

Regardless of the perspective, you choose to take, the vital thing is to remember that the Nordic people greatly valued courage, honor, freedom, individuality, growth, and development. Also, those of us who feel a calling to join the path of Asatru will have to experience the belief system only in the current, modern-day scenario. Therefore, being able to practice the Old Norse religion, the way it existed during the Viking Age, is impossible.

The critical point is that your connection to Asatru must be deep. It calls for a commitment, and it should go beyond learning about Odin, Thor, and other deities. Wearing a miniature of Thor's hammer around your neck is not enough. You will have to learn to live the life of a true Norse pagan.

Asatru Religious Structure

The Gothar is the name for the collective priesthood in Asatru. A single priest is a Gothi (male) or a Gythia (female). The word Gothar translates to: "Those who speak the godly tongue." The Gothar is based on the location and region in which you reside, but you are free to follow any Gothi.

Ceremonies performed by the Gothar are open to the public. Official ceremonies are called blot ('blood'). These are sacrificial ceremonies in which you make an offering to the gods in return for a gift. There's debate as to whether the ceremony should be called a blot if there is no blood in the sacrifice. In that instance, many opt for the term 'faining' instead of blot.

Similar to other paths of Paganism, the solstice and the equinox are days of celebration. However, the Norse don't celebrate the seasons in the same way as us. Instead of each season, there is summer and half-summer, winter and half-winter, because they see half of the year like winter and half as summer. There are four main ceremonies each year:

Jolablot ("yule-blot") is the winter ceremony to honor the goddess Freya. Before Christianization, the Yule was celebrated in January and not December, making this the half-winter celebration.

Sigrblot ("victory-blot") is held on sumardagurinn fyrsti, or summer solstice.

Thingblot ("assembly-blot") is a summer celebration that honors the laws, things (which are meetings or assemblies), and human society.

Veturnattablot (winter-nights-blot") is held on the Winter Solstice in honor of Odin.

Asatru is made of kindreds, or local groups of worship, similar to a community church. They can be family members, friends, or neighbors, as long as they practice Asatru and perform ceremonies and rituals together. These groups may or may not be affiliated with national organizations.

Though Asatru does have gods and practices that are followed, it's also open to the user's interpretation and choice of how they choose to practice. Asatru doesn't follow any specific scriptures or dogma, though many base their teachings on the Poetic Edda and Havamal.

Heathenry Vs. Asatru

Heathenry is a new religious movement known by multiple other terms, including Heathenism, Germanic Neopaganism, or contemporary Germanic Paganism. It was developed in Europe in the early 20th century and is based on pre-Christian beliefs followed by the Germanic tribes from the Iron Age until the Early Middle Ages.

Heathenry is an attempt to revive and reconstruct ancient belief systems using remaining evidence from folklore, history, and archeology. It is a polytheistic belief system that focuses on a pantheon of gods, goddesses, and deities from the pre-Christian era of the Germanic regions. The followers of this new religious movement have adopted the cosmological perspectives from ancient societies and tribes. They believe in animism too, or that the cosmos, including the natural world we see around us, are filled with spirits and other divine beings and creatures.

"Heathens," as the followers call themselves, believe in a system of ethics based on loyalty, personal integrity, and honor. Beliefs in the afterlife are varied but this topic does not get much attention among the Heathens.

Practitioners are trying to understand and revive forgotten belief systems by using one or more of the following sources:

Old Norse texts related to Iceland, including the *Poetic Edda* and *Prose Edda*.

Old English recordings such as Beowulf.

German texts of the Middle Ages such as *Nibelungenlied*.

Archeological evidence throws light on the pre-Christian age of northern Europe.

Folklore-based stories and tales are collectively referred to as "Lore" by Heathens.

Heathenry believers perform sacrificial rites and rituals referred to as "blots," where a variety of libations and food are offered to their deities. Most of the rituals include a ceremony called symbel, which consists of offering a toast of an alcoholic beverage to the gods. Some practitioners also perform rituals to achieve an altered state of reality through visions and wisdom from the invisible spiritual beings and deities. The most popular of these rituals include the seiðr and galdr.

While some practitioners indulge in these rituals individually, some Heathens perform the ceremonies in little groups called "kindreds" or "hearths." The group rituals are usually conducted in open spaces or buildings constructed specifically for this purpose.

Oaths

An important aspect of Asatru is oaths. As can be seen in the previous section, the perspective on hospitality is also considered a key virtue in Asatru. The same is true about making oaths.

Oaths are an extension of the virtues of truth and honor.

Let's look at what an oath is. In the perspective of Asatru, an oath is a promise. It is a guarantee. Upholding an oath is more than just remaining truthful, it is a display of honor and integrity.

In Asatru, an oath holds the weight of a vow.

In my experience, because of the weight that oaths hold, you should not easily make them, nor should they be easily broken.

In general society, honesty and integrity are quite important. They instill trust and strengthen friendships, and while it is important to stick to your promises, they don't hold the same weight as an oath.

For the most part, and with few exceptions, promises can be broken without lasting consequences. Your friends and family might be upset with you for a bit, but it generally isn't anything an apology can't fix.

With oaths, it is completely different. Breaking an oath means dishonoring yourself and could tarnish your reputation within the community.

Asatru Worship

The heathen perspective of worship is quite complicated. There isn't one single way to worship the gods or your ancestors. There is no right way to worship the gods. It all depends on you and how you choose to practice and worship.

That being said, Asatru practitioners worship in a few common ways. One of these ways is through offerings to the gods and their ancestors.

Ancestor veneration is also a common worship practice. Ancestors are quite an important part of Asatru, and it is believed that the dead remain in our lives and often confer blessings on the community and their loved ones.

Therefore, they are revered by their descendants.

Asatru practitioners are can practice worship by living their lives according to the NNV and by honoring the gods through their lifestyles. For example, I often worship by donating to charity and trying my best to improve my relationships with others.

I also worship by celebrating spiritual holidays.

The key point here is that, as Asatru practitioners, we have the freedom to worship as we wish, as long as it is done respectfully and with dignity.

The perspective of worship within general society is as varied and open-ended as it is in Asatru. Practices of worship differ and are heavily dependent on the culture and religion of the area. The worship practices within Hinduism are very different from Christianity.

A major difference between Asatru worship and other religions is the presence of a prescribed dogma and scripture, such as the Bible or the Torah. Most religions have strict practices and methods of worship that are shared across communities, regions, and countries.

While the methods and practices differ, I would argue that the perspective of worship is the same. Both Asatru and Abrahamic religions worship as a means to thank their god or gods and honor these deities.

Similarly, not all Asatruars believe in the physical existence of Odin and the rest of the Æsir. They believe that gods, in essence, are divine energies and higher powers that influence one's life and nurture their spiritual self. They do not have a specific physical form, nor do they have specific "powers." Of course, to connect with a god, they can choose to do so using any way they see fit, but in essence, the belief in the Norse gods isn't rooted in their physical identity, but in their spiritual identity, which is outlined through the Eddas and shaped and experienced through each individual's spirit. As you know, we all experience connection in different ways, whether it's a human connection or a spiritual connection. That is why it's hard to define the nature of connection with the divine without turning the matter into that of opinion and subjective experiences.

Norse Pagans also believe in the Vaettir, the spirits that reside in the wind, trees, forests, lakes, and mountains. Although, these are not worshipped or prayed to but respected, admired, and connected with. According to the Asatruars, these spirits are the reason we feel connected to and in touch with nature. Nature, after all, is alive in its way, and we are a part of it. It is only natural for us to form spiritual bonds with our surroundings. Vaettir are also thought to be the guardians of the natural world in which they inhabit. Asatru preaches humility, emphasizing that we are guests in the Vaettir's land, and thus must be respectful of the natural world around us.

Freewill and fate also had a place in the concept of destiny for the Norse. The Norse had it that there were three wise women, known as Norns, who lived in the Well of Urd. The Norns are generally called the goddesses of destiny and were believed to carve the fortunes of those to be born. Again, through that process, the past influenced the future. The Norns would carve the future of all beings; humans, gods, and even salamanders, into the tree. Whatever they formed anyone into was what they would become in the Yggdrasil, but that was not the only thing they could become. Their destinies could be changed.

That was a major deviation from the ancient Greek concept of fate that confers absolute powers unto fate. Since the dewdrops from Yggdrasil could alter what had been written about a thing, a human, a god, or any other being, it could cause a change to occur from the Tree and change their destiny from the initial form they were carved into. For the most part, however, most of the beings with the power to change their destinies only used the power passively by merely influencing the flow of the Water of Destiny into the Well of Destiny.

Some, however, took their destinies into their own hands, so to speak, shaping it more powerfully and actively. The system of things and interaction between beings also played a role in shaping fortunes. Some beings were able to exert influence on this process and rewrite their destinies, allowing dewdrops from the cosmos to change the composition of the Water of Destiny as it affected them.

From all the available information about the Norse view of destiny, life course didn't necessarily obey the writings or Norns, and there was also no life completely and preordained by the Norns. In summary, it wasn't possible to have absolute free will or be free from fate altogether. At the same time, the Norse concept of destiny wasn't unalterably binding. Thus, their lives resided somewhere in-between.

Difference Between Asatru and Wicca

Asatru is one of the sects of Heathenism. "Tru" literally means "faith" in the Icelandic language, and therefore, Asatru translates to Aesir's faith or belief. As you already know, Aesir were gods from one of the tribes of deities worshipped in Norse Paganism. Asatru practitioners are called Asatruar. The primary focus of Asatru is on the Nordic gods and goddesses of Scandinavia, but Asatruars worship other deity groups, including the Vanir, elves, dwarfs, and valkyries.

Another name for Asatru is Vanatru, or those who venerate the Vanir tribe of Nordic deities. A smaller group of Asatruars venerates and worships the jotnar (or jotunn) and refers to their community as Rokkatru. Forn Sed or the "Old Way" is another common term used to replace Asatru. Most right-wing people prefer to call their belief system Odinism, Wodenism, *etc.*

Asatru emerged before Christianity in northern Europe. The citizens practiced different religions specific to the territory. Among them, Asatru was popular in Scandinavia, Germany, the Netherlands, and England. It is an indigenous faith of the inhabitants of these regions. The term Asatru, from the Norse spoken in ancient Scandinavia, can be translated to "belief in Gods." Norsemen referred to the various practices attached to their faith as Asatru. Asatru was often alluded to as heathens. It is often linked to Wotanism, Germanic Paganism, or Woodanism. Popular books detailing the wisdom of Asatru are the Eddas and the Sagas.

Asatru is a faith with multiple deities. Many of them, like Thor, have gained significance in popular culture. Asatru was systematically destroyed over hundreds of years, and its non-Christian practices were repressed. The monolithic nature of the Church demonized Pagan practices and led to the eventual downfall of Asatru. Its teachings and ideas lived on through enduring oral histories, traditions, and folklore. The faith has resurfaced in contemporary times through the Neo-Pagan movement in Europe.

Wicca, also referred to as "pagan witchcraft" or "earth religion," is a relatively new religious movement that was only introduced in 1954 by Gerald Gardner – a British civil servant. Wicca draws its knowledge from various other pagan religions and practices – from voodoo to Satanism, Greek mythology, Celtic mythology, and many other faiths.

Nowadays, Wicca is seeing a fair amount of growth – mainly from teenagers who reject the idea of Christian Paternalism. While it would be stereotypical to say that Wiccans are spell-casting Satanists, indeed, the two religious movements could not be any different.

Known as "The Old Religion" or "The Craft," Wicca works on the belief that all reality is something divine. As a result, the Wiccans will worship everything in the natural world, considering it a breathing organism. In Wicca, people are revered as gods and goddesses – since each one of them has a particular role in maintaining a balance.

Some would say that Wicca is a feminist version of neo-Paganism since the Supreme Being is considered to be a goddess (for instance, the Triple Goddess of the Moon). This forms a sharp contrast with the Christian worldview that places a man at the top.

Wicca adheres to one supreme ethical rule – and that is the Wiccan Rede. The rule says: "if it harms none, do as ye Will." As long as no one is harmed in the process, there's no reason why you should not do as you wish. This code is generally seen as a declaration to act freely while taking responsibility for what you do.

Wiccans believe that moral and religious truths are ultimately relative – which sets them apart from the satanic activities – with which they are continuously associated. They also do not think that Jesus is the only truth – and the truth can be anything that you wish to believe in.

Wiccans also believe in the "Law of Threefold Return." In other words, every action that you ever take will be returned threefold – mirroring the idea of karma.

As a person that might not be familiar with the witchcraft of Wicca, the word "magic" may bring a variety of things to your mind: a magician popping out a rabbit from his hat, wizards chanting "Wingardium Leviosa" and making other people float, or individuals making other people disappear by simply snapping their fingers. This is what Hollywood movies have taught us so far.

However, people who practice magic know that this is not as flashy as pop culture makes it look. For them, magic is very subtle – but more powerful than anyone could ever think.

In the Wiccan world, magic is spelled "magick," with a "k." This was British occultist Aleister Crowley's idea so that Wiccan magic could be distinguished from the magic used by popular illusionists or stage magicians.

Many people perceive Aleister Crowley to be the "wickedest man on earth" – and since he is a follower of the Wicca, then implicitly, the religion should be evil as well. However, the truth is relatively far from that. The aim of magic in Wicca is to improve a person's circumstances, particularly when it comes to love, wealth, or health.

For instance, Wiccans may work up some spells for a better-paid job, the speedy recovery of an ailment, or finding a life partner. However, a common purpose of magic is for protection or "cleaning" someone's life of the negative influences.

Furthermore, Wiccans do not practice magic only for personal gain. Some witches will work for the benefit of other people that they know or that might be in the need of their help. For example, those who are part of a particular Wiccan circle may work together to send positive energy towards an ailing family member, acquaintance – or a whole group that has survived an earthquake.

The magic is done through various traditions, influences, and approaches. A witch may use anything from spells and charms to incantations, rituals, dancing, divination, potion-making, and dances to make a spell work.

Wiccans also generally use natural tools when doing their magic – such as crystals, herbs, shells, and so on. Since the attention of the witches is on the ongoing natural process, they are required to use tools and mediums that have not gone through human processing yet.

Wicca is a customized practice of ancient witchcraft. The term Wicca is now applied to the modern tradition of Pagan witchcraft and Paganism as a whole. While "witchcraft" and "Wicca" are commonly used synonymously, there are also practices of ancient witchcraft that are not based on Wicca. Wicca was used initially to categorize the practice of witchcraft as a religion. However, popular Western representations also adopted the term to encompass what may previously have been considered natural magic or "white witchcraft." When people refer to themselves as Wiccan, they are usually discussing the sort of religious witchcraft they perform. The media frequently portrays female witches as young girls, but in actuality, witchcraft is performed by men and women of any age. In modern times, it has become a festival based on nature worship. People who belong to the Wiccan identity engage in rituals based on seasonal festivals like the solstice and equinox. Deities of male and female genders are venerated, and these rituals include herbalism and natural elements. There are moral and ethical laws that govern the Wiccan, and they believe in the afterlife. However, all these practices can differ across sects.

Wicca is a modern resurgence of pre-Christian faiths, and some members claim to be part of families directly descended from primitive witches. Wiccans can form groups for a practice called covens, or they may practice alone. Mostly, Wiccans perform their faith in multiple ways; however, duotheism, or the worship of two gods of the male and female gender, is common. The male god may be referred to as the "Horned God" and the latter as the "Mother Goddess." People from the unorthodox sect who only believe in a female God are called the "Dianic Wicca." There are polytheistic, pantheistic, and atheistic Wiccans as well. Such Wiccans show respect to deities as a mere symbolic aspect of the religion but do not consider them to exist as supernatural beings.

As the primary guide on morality, the Wiccan Rede is at the heart of the religion's spirituality. Etymologically, "rede" translates to "council" or "advice" in ancient German. The main Rede can be translated to, "As ye harm none, do what ye will," and it means "Do what you want to do, but do not harm anything in the process." This means the basic tenets of the Wicca – to act fairly and ensure everyone's wellbeing around you. The thought that actions have larger consequences than ourselves is connected to the idea of nature as well. Coexistence is a primary philosophy – humans exist with the natural elements around them, which must be respected equally.

A significant law among Wiccans is "The Rule of Threefold Return." This law is similar to Hindu karmic theory and argues that your action will return to you three times more than you originally planned, so you will suffer if you act with bad intentions. A proper Wiccan must focus on doing good actions to avoid suffering in life. This rule of the "threefold" is ritually revealed to initiates during the second stage of induction. The ritual consists of the initiator whipping the initiate, and the former returns the action three times on the initiator that whipped them. This rule was published in Gerald Gardner's book *High Magic Aid*. Another Wiccan called Raymond Buckland produced a different definition of the Rule of Threefold Return in 1986. He clarified the karmic content of this law and argued that it is not merely a Wiccan code of conduct. He attached a larger significance to actions by placing them in a supernatural realm of justice.

The performance of rituals may be conducted in specific places of worship and magic, which are called altars. When Wiccan practice was limited to covens, there was a single altar for coven gatherings. However, with the rise of individual practitioners, altars began to be built for personal use.

The Moon is essential to Wiccans and many holidays revolve around its phases. Solar equinoxes, solstices, the four natural elements (water, air, fire, earth), and initiation rituals are some other elements celebrated by the religion.

"Esbats" and "sabbats" constitute two major Wiccan festivals. There are thirteen full-moon esbats and the cycle of eight sabbats. The former takes place when the moon is full, and the latter at intervals within the "wheel of the year."

The Wheel of the Year is a periodic cycle of annual festivals (occurring seasonally) practiced by many western Pagans and composed of the year's major solar cycles and their midpoints. Though each festivals' terms differ from one Pagan practice to another, syncretic associations generate a commonality of reference, especially in Wicca, to all the festivals that relate to solar events, which occur quarterly by the calendar as "quarter days" and the events in-between as "cross-quarter days." The various groups of modern Paganism often differ as to each festival's exact date, depending on variations such as the phase of the moon and the geographical hemisphere location.

Monitoring the seasonal cycle was essential to several peoples, both ancient and modern. New Pagan festivals that depend on the Wheel of the Year focus on folk customs, independent of real historical practices. To Wiccans, each holiday is often alluded to as the Sabbat, based on Gerald Gardner's argument that when the Jewish term "Shabbat" was merged with the rhetoric of heretical celebrities, this word was transmitted down from the Middle Ages.

In certain beliefs of western Pagan cosmology, all occurrences are known to be cyclical, with time as a continuous period of development and withdrawal connected to the periodic death and resurrection of the Sun. This loop is often used as a micro-and-macrocosm of several life cycles in a tremendous sequence of Universe cycles. Customarily, the periods that fall on the annual period's landmarks represent the start and the center of the four major seasons. They are thought to be important and are also the venue for big community festivals. These eight events are the most popular period for cultural festivities.

Even though the "major" holidays are typically quarter-days and cross-quarter-days, some festivals are often celebrated during the year, particularly among non-Wiccan practices such as polytheistic restoration associations and in keeping with other indigenous customs.

In Wicca and rituals influenced by it, gatherings related to solar trends have traditionally been immersed in solar myths and meaning based on the light's life cycles. Such synchronization with nature links witchcraft closely to the essence of nature. Likewise, the Wiccan esbats are historically related to the celestial cycles. Together they reflect the most popular celebrations of Wiccan-influenced types of Neo-Paganism, particularly in modern Witchcraft communities.

Another important ritual is the Wiccan Funerary Rite. Each funeral can differ from sect to coven, yet they share some features, especially the principle of ensuring environmentally-conscientious burials. The dead person is laid to rest in a natural atmosphere, wrapped in a shroud made of organic cloth to allow natural and quick decomposition. The earth's divinity is respected by the body's return to it and the nutrition it provides for new life forms to grow through death. Sometimes burial outside or in a natural setting is not permitted by law. Wiccans may bury the ashes after cremation in such a case. There are special ways of honoring the dead, such as memorializing them by distributing some ashes to loved ones. This allows for different ways of remembrance.

Wiccans believe in the afterlife that leads to reincarnation. When someone dies, their spirit lives on by being birthed as a new person. It is believed that these reincarnated souls have a chance to meet their friends and family of previous lives. Death is not seen as salvation from the earth. Reincarnation symbolizes the pleasure a person can achieve by being born multiple times on earth. The experience of life itself is a gift. Living is related to learning and gathering knowledge; however, a world beyond constant reincarnation is called "Summerland." This supernatural place is also known as the "Land of Youth" and is where spirits seek salvation once they have completed the cycle of death and reincarnation. It is the realm of joy, bliss, and ultimate transcendence. It is imagined as a place with immense greenery, abundant in beauty and peace. Spirits may also rest here to reconnect with those they have lost.

The funeral service itself is an expression of respect for the deceased person's wishes. There may be rules which disallow non-Wiccans from participating in the ceremony. In contemporary times, relatives and close ones are generally allowed to be a part of the final farewell. The service is divided into two parts – the funeral ritual and the burial of the body. The funeral ritual is presided over by a Priest or a Priestess who directs the ceremony with the ushers' or assistants' help. The altar is used for laying down the body, and the ritual setting is cleared of all other objects. The place is made fit for rituals by the Priestess, and the attendees wait outside the sacred circle. Incantations and spiritual chants serve as forces of magic. Speaking is essential; mourners and Priests may address the deceased and express parting sentiments for their journey into the afterlife. The next part of the funeral is the burial. The body is made fit for burial by the direction of the Priestess. After the burial is complete, all are invited to recall precious memories with the deceased and pray for their peaceful rest. All these rituals of sharing and expressed intimacy are a means to maintain the strength offered by the community. There may be specific prayers and ritual chants that can be found on Wiccan coven resources and sites for reference.

Wiccan philosophies and rituals have been adopted by the "Goddess Spirituality Movement." This movement is primarily based on celebrating anti-patriarchal gods. The community consists of people who have abandoned the idea of a male supreme deity. The Goddess is female, and her femininity is divine and supreme.

Wicca also shares similarities with Druidry. As already noted, like Wicca, Druidry is based on a connection with nature through outdoor settings and also considers the environment as being divine. Their rituals are deeply embedded in sustaining and seeking further connection with an all-powerful nature. The Druids and Wiccans see themselves as the guardians of the earth and stress its conservation. However, Wicca is not as Celtic as Druidry. Magic or sorcery is seminal to the Wiccan tradition, unlike Druidry. Artistic expressions like poetry, music, and performance are considered fertile paths for spiritual rejuvenation.

One salient principle central to a Wiccan lifestyle is that it offers an autonomy of faith practice by maintaining the legitimacy of diverse practices. Wiccans believe in consequentialism, as illustrated by ethical and moral supernatural laws. The belief in actions loaded with karmic consequences fosters a sense of empathy. Such principles offer a legitimate counter to false ideas about witchcraft as something evil and dark. Traditionally, witches have been seen as dangerous and unreliable. However, the resurgence of Wicca has allowed for a new way of experiencing faith. The neo-Wiccan academia has allowed for women's empowerment by stressing the strength of the feminine form. In 2002, a research project called "Enchanted Feminism: The Reclaiming Witches of San Francisco" showed that some Wiccans were members of the second wave of feminism. North America is a good place to study the prevailing ideas of feminism within Neo-Pagan religious groups. As a religious movement, Wicca has become intermeshed with larger political struggles and has provided an alternate lifestyle of activism and care for its members.

Ragnarok

Ragnarok means "The Doom of the Gods." This is the name that the Norse gave to the ultimate end of their cosmos and then their re-creation. The word Ragnarok is a play on words, but we'll look at that a little later, first let's look at the story itself.

In Norse mythology, Ragnarok referred to the end of the world. Sometime in the future, when Ragnarok took place, the world would suffer a devastating and long winter that would be three years long and with no summers. Fighting would erupt throughout the Norse world. Family members would attack each other. Then, earthquakes and other cataclysmic events would take place. The earth would be plunged into darkness and crack open at the tectonic plates. Next, the gods and giants would begin a long battle.

As Ragnarök built to a close, the gods would fight with a wolf and a serpent. The serpent's venom would kill Thor. The wolf would swallow Odin. The world would be engulfed in fire and then drowned in flood.

After Ragnarok, the earth would rise out of the sea and be green and beautiful once more. The sons of the gods would return. Only two humans would survive, and they would repopulate the world. Unlike in the Christian end-of-world story, the world formed would contain both kind people and dangerous foes.

As one reads about Ragnar Lothbrok's legend, one can see how many of these gods, people, and animals were incorporated into the stories handed down by the Norse storytellers, the Skalds.

The mythology was more than a collection of exciting stories for the Norsemen of that time. They chose how to live based on their views of what the gods did. They celebrated their victories in honor of the god Odin. And they incorporated information about the gods into their oral histories.

The Norse didn't believe Ragnarök had already happened. Most of the stories in Norse mythology happened in the past, but Ragnarök is one of the few that hasn't happened yet. The Norse didn't know when it was going to happen, but they knew exactly what would happen. A lot of other cultures have stories about the end of the world, but the Norse version is very detailed. A lot of the gods and creatures you've already learned about come back in Ragnarök.

The word Ragnarök means "Fate of the Gods." It's the story of what happens to the cosmos and the gods when the Norns decide that it's time for the world to end. The Norse believed that since the world started with fire and ice, it would also end with it.

When Ragnarök begins, there will be a long and cold winter. The Earth will be covered in snow and ice just like Niflheim, and the sun will disappear. Humans will go hungry because no food will grow. Skoll and Hati, two wolves who have been trying to catch the sun and the moon since the beginning of time, will catch Sol and Mani. After they take these two lights, the stars will also disappear. There will be no more night sky or even a sky in the daytime. Everything will be pitch black.

Then, at last, Yggdrasil will shake. When Yggdrasil shakes, the mountains will fall, and the monsters that had been locked away from humans will be free. Fenrir will break his chains, and Jormungand will jump out of the ocean in the sky and fall to Earth.

When Fenrir and Jormungand are free, Loki will also be able to break out of his chains. Remember that Loki was locked up after Baldur died. Since he was chained up by the gods, Loki will betray them and command an army of giants. The giants want to destroy the gods and the cosmos. Ragnarök is when they get the chance to do it.

Ragnarok will be heralded by the crowing of the Aesir cock in Vahalla as well as the crowing of Hel's cock in the Hell-Ways. Fjalar, the cock of the giants, also will crow, and the hound of Hel will bay far down below Yggdrasil in Niflheim. The world will descend into wickedness for three years, and this will be followed by a long, snowy winter. No warmth will come from the sun, which will be swallowed by the wolf called Skoll. Another wolf will swallow the moon. The stars will be extinguished and earthquakes all around cause the world, even the mountains, to tremble. The Fenris Wolf and Loki both will be freed, and the Midgard Serpent will cause the waters of the sea to rear up and wash over the land.

Loki will steer a ship made up of the nails of dead men. Rime-Thursar and other giants will follow. All of these wicked creatures - Loki, the Fenris Wolf, the Midgard Serpent, the giant Rym, the Rime-Thursar - will be free to raise their hordes for battle. The Aesir also prepares for war with the sounding of the Gjallar-Horn. The Gods are roused, and Odin seeks guidance from Mimir's head. The two hosts meet on the field of Vigrid. Odin is first, dressed in his golden armor and brandishing Gungnir, his spear.

Odin and Thor, respectively, prepare to fight the Fenris Wolf and the Midgard Serpent. Thor fights Midgard Serpent and vanquished him, but only walks nine steps more until he falls dead. The Fenris Wolf swallows Odin until God is vanquished. Other Gods among the Aesir die, too. Freyr is vanquished by Surty while Loki and Heimdal slay each other. Surt covers the world in flame and all things on the earth perish. This sets the stage for a new life. A new land rises, young and green. Plants grow without seeds needing to be sewn. The sun and her daughter herald a new day. Those Aesir who did not die return, setting the stage for the All-Father, the governor of everything.

Dreams and prophecies had long existed and told the destruction of the cosmos and everything that lived in it. Once the first event came to pass, which was Baldur being killed, the gods were forced to look at the fact that they couldn't escape their destiny. Odin began to gather the best human warriors to help him fight in his last battle against the giants. Even though they prepared, they knew that there was no way that they could stop their demise.

The human population abandoned their normal way of life and fell into a deep depression. The same could be said for the gods. Many broke oaths and fell short of many of their expectations. Three winters would come one right after another. There would be no summer between them. This devastating darkness and frigidity were prophesied as the Fimbulwinter, The Great Winter.

Death and the Afterlife

There were never any actual Norse doctrines concerning what happened to people after they died. Even though there aren't any certain views on life after death, some sources perceive their afterlife as something other than chaos. There are some discernible patterns as to how the Norse people saw death and the afterlife.

The spiritual parts of the deceased were thought to go to a certain otherworld. The most famous one would be that of Valhalla. The people personally chosen by Odin and his Valkyries got to spend their eternity in Valhalla preparing for Ragnarok.

Another hall is Folkvang, ruled by Freya. Sadly, Folkvang, meaning "the field of the people," is only mentioned sparsely in some texts. This means that we don't know what kind of place it was like.

Anybody who died at sea, which was a relatively common occurrence given the seafaring culture, is sometimes said to be taken to the underwater abode of Ran, a giantess.

The most common world that people went to when they died was Hel, which is the underworld, looked over by the goddess Hel. Besides being the general underworld, they also tell us that families would remain together in one place close to the area that they had lived in when living.

The life in the afterlife was much like that of their living life. They practiced magic, slept, fought, caroused, drank, and ate. The differentiation of the different afterlives is blurry, and there isn't one definitive understanding as to how a person gets sent to a specific world.

Some sources also talk about people who die as being reborn as one of their descendants. They are never reborn into a different bloodline. Most of the time, they would be born as somebody in their lineage that was given their name.

Most people today look at the afterlife as a reward or punishment for how they have lived their lives. The Norse people didn't hold these types of views. Salvation and damnation were never a part of their worldview. So, anybody that goes looking for a place similar to Heaven or Hell amongst the afterlife dwellings in Norse belief isn't going to find anything. The words Hell and Hel do come from the same root word, but the location and name are the only things the two have in common.

There is one text that makes mention of an afterlife that does punish people when they die: Nastrond, which means "shore of corpses." It contains a north-facing gate, a ceiling that drips poison, and a snake coils along the floor. The problem is that the poem is heavily influenced by Christianity.

Norse mythology doesn't have a lot of detail emphasizing what happens to the dead. However, literary sources of Old Norse contain some references here and there which help to understand Norse concepts about death and the afterlife. As it should be expected in cases like this, some contradictions exist in the positions of the historians that have studied them.

In Norse mythology, the dead usually went to a place known as Valhalla, which means the hall of the fallen. It was Odin, together with his Valkyries, that would choose those who would dwell here as fallen heroes and who would be brought back to participate in the final battle of Ragnarok, which would destroy the gods and the cosmos.

Another place that the dead went to was Folkvang, which was the hall of the goddess Freya, which means the field of the people (or the field of the warriors). This was where she welcomed some of the dead. Those who died at sea would go to the giantess Ran, who would take them to her underwater abode.

Anyone who ended up in Hel continued to live a normal life, virtually doing all the things they had enjoyed before their death; this place was not used to punish the dead.

There is no clear demarcation in the descriptions regarding the abodes of the dead and the facts are hazy as to who would go to anyone particular realm and why, and who determined where each would go after his or her death.

The Rebirth of the Dead

The concept of reincarnation is present in the Old Norse afterlife. The Norse are said to have believed that the dead would be reborn back into the family of a relative. No one can explain the process clearly. However, children were usually named after loved ones who had passed, with the hope that the dead would be reincarnated in the child who was named after him or her.

Norse literature sometimes described dead ancestors as elves. The only logic here would be that the dead would become elves since Norse mythology already says that every living thing that had a spiritual presence could change its being.

No Punishment and Reward After Death

The Norse did not have any of the common beliefs today concerning reward or punishment after death. There were no concepts such as salvation or damnation in the worldview of the Norse.

The Helgafjell

Helgafjell means the holy mountain, one of the places that occupied the Norse concept of the afterlife. After the death of a Norse clansperson, he or she would go up to this mountain, a place so holy that before people could look towards it, they would have to wash their face. But the dead who resided in Helgafjell could lead a normal existence, just like those who lived life on earth.

The Soul

Beliefs concerning the soul deserve consideration when analyzing the Norse concept of the afterlife. The Norse believed the soul to be the last breath taken by a person in the process of dying. This means that life evaporates when a person breathes their last "soul." Another understanding of the soul suggested that it was an immaterial part of the human being that was immortal and would leave the body when a person became unconscious, either momentarily or when life evaporated and the body began to decay.

The concept of souls for the Norse was quite different from what we understand today. According to the Norse, the soul was divided into four parts:

Hamr was one's physical appearance. It could change and be associated with shapeshifting.

Hugr was the person's character and personality which followed them after death.

Fylgja was their companion animal that reflected their hugr. Stronger individuals had stronger totems.

Hamingja was the person's success in life formed by the hugr and would be passed down to close family members, either in good or bad omen.

The soul would split after death and each of the four aspects ventures into different directions. This was not controlled by the will of the gods, and it seemed to be something more personal; therefore, less information is known about it. The *hugr* is what is thought to be what passed onto a newborn baby in the community, and thus the person's character would show itself in the newborn.

As with most historical sources from the time, they were heavily influenced by Christian writings, but what we do know from the scripts is a general overview of the destination of the souls:

Valhalla: Known as the hall of heroes or Odin's hall. Here the warriors of both men and women would meet like old friends to drink, celebrate, and fight in preparation for Ragnarök.

Folkvangr: This is the field of the people watched over by the fertility goddess Freyja. It was the land of peace and rest.

Hel: Located in the ice world of Niflheim and presided over by the goddess Hel, most people went here after death. Most likely a post-Christian adaptation of the underworld as this was not a concept shown before the conversion.

Realm of Rán: also called the Coral Caves of Rán, this giantess would watch over the treasure and sailors befallen to the seas.

The Burial Mound: some souls never left their graves. If they were prepared correctly with all of their treasures and belongings, they would stay in that vicinity and were known as ghosts.

Runes

The word "runes" basically means "secret whisper." Of course, there are other variations of translation when we look at different languages, but this is the generally accepted meaning. Even though the Elder Futhark is known as the first runic alphabet, we have also learned of its use in magic, or 'magick.' The runes themselves can be looked at in the form of letters, but they were more so sounds that formed the word or sentence or to be more precise, each one had meaning.

The ancient Germanic system for writing used a runic alphabet. The runes worked similar to letters, but they are very different from how we view letters today. Each one was analogous to a pictographic symbol that represented some principle. When one wrote a rune, they invoked the power for which the image stood. The runes each had a name that hinted at a magical significance. They called their alphabets "futharks," which corresponds to the first six runes. Traditionally, runes would be carved into metal, bone, wood, stone, or other hard surfaces.

There are many arguments about the details of runic writing, but there is a general agreement in its outline. The runes are believed to have come from some of the Old Italic alphabets used among Mediterranean people during the first century. Other early Germanic symbols were influential in the runic script development as well.

The earliest runic inscription can be found on a brooch that was made in an area north of what is now Germany, in 50 CE. The inscription is debated, and many are divided about whether the inscription is Roman or runic. The earliest inscriptions that aren't disputed were found on a comb from Vimose and on a spearhead that came from Norway. Both date to around 160 CE. The earliest carving of the whole futhark is on the Kylver stone located in Gotland, Sweden. This dates to around 400 CE.

Even though scholars have tried to discover where the runic alphabet was derived from, the ancient Germanic people never believed that the runes ever came from a mundane source such as the Old Italic alphabet. They didn't see the runes as something that was invented. They have always been and pre-existed Odin himself until he was able to discover them.

The runes of the Old Norse mythology were carved on the tree Yggdrasil by the Norns. This helps to prove the belief that when somebody wrote a rune, they released the power of what was being written.

It could be presumed that after Odin discovers the runes that he then was the one who gave the knowledge of the runes to the first human runemaster.

With the importance that the Norse put into words as a whole, believing that each one held its power, we can begin to understand the awe the rune-masters inspired and why the ability to read and inscribe the runes was held in such regard. They believed that words shape reality and runes shape words; therefore, they must shape some of the reality-altering power of the spoken word.

The actual casting of the runes was done as we would cast dice in a board game today and is not to be confused with spellcasting, which we will discuss later. Castings can involve one or many runes, depending on the experience of the practitioner, and when we discuss 'layouts' in a bit, you will see how much variation there can be in everyone.

Looking at cave paintings or the wall paintings in the Great Pyramid of Giza, we instantly see what appears to be almost historical records. The images were painted to show exact descriptions or what was seen through the artist's eyes. They are representations of events or moments that someone wanted to portray to another.

Runes, on the other hand, were seen as a way of encapsulating the forces of nature, our existence, or the powers of the gods. Even though they were built on an alphabetical standing, they were still seen to embody so much more. In the wrong hands, they could be dangerous; but when the rune-masters and the lucky few who believed in the good they could bring harnessed what they had to give, then things like the past, present, and future became something that could be tapped into and used.

Magic is an internal entity. It is not about altering the components of our life or making power and fortune fall into our lap. Following the Hollywood narrative of divination, fortune-telling, sorcery, or whatever is the latest blockbuster trend will be detrimental in your search for the true meaning of the Elder Futhark and all it has to offer.

Most of the time, the Norse people used the runes and the magic that they provided for more mundane things than altering the weather or striking down an enemy tribe with illness. It was not about altering reality, per se, but more like giving it and themselves a helping hand. They used it to point them in the right direction, whether that be better hunting grounds or improved fertility.

What Is the Use of Runes?

There are so many things Runes can be used for, especially if you already have experience with cards or crystals. Many Norse Pagans find guidance with the help of Runes during rough patches. With Rune divination, one won't get to foresee the future but may get several different options of what may be coming. The Runes will usually hint toward answers. The caster will still need to work to figure out the details. It is also important to remember that the future is fluid and flexible, so our decisions have the power to affect it and change the outcome.

Another important point to keep in mind is that Rune reading isn't an exact science but a tool to help your intuition clarify possible outcomes.

Apart from divination, Runes are often used as talismans or jewelry. Some Norse Pagans like to carve Runes on their jewelry, whether that's on the metal part or gemstones. There is no wrong way to carve a Rune as long as our intentions are pure.

Others prefer a more active approach to using Runes, so they opt for talismans instead. Talismans are large medallions that have been inscribed with Runes and often have a big stone set in the center. Talismans are often considered alive and conscious by practitioners.

Historically, the best Rune carvers would use their blood or the blood of a sacrificial beast to color their Runes, which would supposedly give them even more power. In actuality, though, any ink or paint can be used according to the carver's preference. Timing, however, is more important. For example, the phases of the moon should be considered. A waxing, waning, or full moon will imbue the Rune with different kinds of powers.

It is ideal if the caster carves their own set of Runes, but a store-bought set can also be used. Handmade Runes tend to be more potent, but it doesn't matter if you find it easier to purchase a set.

The Old Norse used to do Rune inscriptions in odd numbers. However, whoever does the inscription can pick any number they deem important. A runic inscription should read like a story, concluding with the outcome the inscriber wants. Some people chant or sing each Rune's name while carving or inscribing them. That is an option. The focus should be on imbuing the Runes with intention while creating them.

Crafting a Rune Set

Crafting a Rune set will help one get more accurate readings since the Runes will be connected to the caster.

The choice of material is up to the crafter. While oak wood is best, it can be anything from stone to clay to shells. Some are easier to work with, but others might be more spiritually significant to the crafter.

After the material has been decided, it needs, of course, to be acquired. Stones and shells should be flat and rounded (preferably tumbled) and similar in size and shape. The easiest way to cut tiles from wood is to find a fallen branch and slice it into tiles. Whatever the material, make sure that it is legal to harvest it from an area. Don't forget to make an offering to the spirits of the land. In the case of wood, it is better to opt for a fallen branch as the wood from a living tree should only be cut when there aren't any other available sources. The offering you make should be safe for both the flora and the fauna of the area.

Deciding how to write the Runes is the next thing to do. Modern ways include wood burning, painting, carving, or inking. To empower the Runes even further, blood can be used to tint or mixed with other pigments.

After the Runes are drawn, they should be consecrated. The methods differ from region to region, but the majority of Rune casters agree that they should be consecrated after being made.

The ritual space should be prepared, cleansed, and smudged. The Rune caster then invokes the Rune deities, ancestors, and other spirits they may want to present. The Runes are then laid out on a cloth that will be burned afterward. The Rune crafter offers a drink to the deities and then finally asks them to lend their powers of purification.

The Runes are washed, not soaked, in pure consecrated water. Another smudging blend of purifying herbs is then burned and dedicated to the deities. Then, each Rune is passed through the smoke while its name is spoken aloud and returned to the cloth.

Using a brush or quill, the Runes are painted or tinted (if carved) with the pigment of your choice. While each Rune is painted, its name is chanted. After all the Runes are painted or tinted, the sacred space is taken down, and the Runes are allowed to dry undercover.

After the Runes have dried, the sacred space is erected again, and the pigment sealed with a sealant of choice. While the Runes are being polished or sealed, a galdr should be sung to them.

After sealing, the Rune crafter holds each Rune over their heart and connects with them.

Rune Casting

Now, onto casting the runes. Some magical traditions do the process by casting or tossing the runes onto a white cloth, which provides a clear background for reading the runes and a magical boundary extremely useful during the casting process.

Some casters do it directly on the ground. As the one who will be doing the casting, you have the freedom to pick the method you want. Once the casting session ends, get a small box or pouch where you can store them.

You can cast runes using any of the many methods available. Each one of them is as valid as the next. A couple of layouts are currently popular with modern rune casters.

Like other divination methods, rune casting addresses one particular issue and lets you look for the things that could influence it from your past and present. For instance, you may want to do a 3-rune cast by pulling three, one at a time, from the pouch. You can then place them side-by-side on a white cloth.

The first rune you pulled out represents the general overview of your situation. The second one is for the challenges and obstacles in your way, while the last one gives you the potential paths you can take in response.

Here is how a basic rune casting session would usually start:

Lay out your runes on the cloth, all facing up to make sure that the set is complete. After that, you can put them back inside the pouch.

Place your hand inside the pouch and mix them up as best as you can. While doing so, concentrate on your question.

Pick up a couple of runes that will depend on the casting method you chose and toss them onto the cloth.

Use the runes that landed face up to do your reading. If you do not have enough runes facing upward to do your reading, you can choose to re-cast and start over again, re-cast the runes that landed face-down or leave the spaces in the spread blank.

How to Pick the Runes from the Casting Cloth

Once the runes are on the casting cloth, the next thing that may cross your mind is how to figure out which ones to pick up. Fortunately, there are a couple of ways to do so. The first involves picking a spot on the cloth before you cast them. Then pick up the rune closest to it for the first spot on the spread. After that, pick the one closest next. Continue doing so until all the spaces in your spread are full.

Another way is to imagine a line running down the center of the casting cloth and then pick up the face-up rune that lands closest to it first. If two runes are somewhat the same distance from the line, pick the one closest to you first. The spots in your spread are full; the next step is to read them and figure out their meanings.

How Meditation Can Help with Readings

Suppose you can place yourself into a higher level of thought due to meditation. There, you will immediately discover that, even if you are not actively meditating, your senses are still more aware than ever. Every time you open your senses to the everyday world, you exercise and continuously train your mind to see things differently. You will have other perspectives where you can base your decisions.

Because you are more in tune with your surroundings, you can easily pick up the smaller details you may have otherwise missed, helping you make sense of the runes better. For instance, when you sit down with a person for a rune reading, you can get a grasp of his or her personality. You can read other people better so you can give them a more accurate interpretation of the runes.

Here is a sample scenario. You have a friend who is going for a job interview next week, and he wants to know if he will get the job. Being his friend, you already know that he is the kind of person who will tense up during an interview but is also very qualified.

You also know the job your friend is interviewing for involves dealing with other people; so, he needs to work on his people skills. In that case, you may cast your runes. Perhaps Uruz is the most important. Uruz is a rune for power –but it is one out of people's control. It can also mean that success is nearby.

Typically, you can tell your friend that success is near, but it comes with a power he has no control over. Also, you are not sure when this power will come. If you meditate before the reading and are in a more mindful state, you can sense your friend's attitude about the job. If you feel that your friend is in control, the power without control likely comes with the job.

Paths of the Norse Faith

The forms of Norse Paganism practiced nowadays are as diverse as the Old Norse religion used to be. Due to how the Internet has fundamentally changed society, it is easier to adhere to a different path from that of your local community.

However, you don't need to have a community to become a Norse Pagan. You can choose from several paths. You will find the one best suited to you. Some of those paths are solitary, while others are community-based. Some branches prefer to be as true to tradition as possible, while others prefer to change and adapt to the times. Others are more philosophical.

One doesn't even need to follow one of the most well-known branches. Being a Norse Pagan means being true to yourself. You should practice the way you prefer, even if you need to make up your practices. To start, you should get acquainted with the surviving texts and then decide which path suits you best.

And remember, if none of the following paths call to you, there are several other options to choose from. You just have to explore further to find them.

Some of the most common (but not all) paths of Norse Paganism today are these:

Fórn Siðr

Fórn Siðr means "the old way." The Old Norse, as mentioned, didn't consider their beliefs and way of life a religion. With the coming of

Christianity (which was "the new way"), the Old Norse religion began to be referred to as Fórn Siðr, the 'old way' or 'old customs.'

Norse Paganism

Christians tend to refer to any nonbeliever as a pagan, usually with the word carrying a negative connotation. Paganism usually refers to any religion other than the three mainstream ones, Judaism, Christianity, and Islam, and usually, in particular, those that predate Christianity.

Heathenry

Norse Paganism practitioners often identify as Heathens and refer to their faith generally as 'Heathenry' as an homage to the old ways before the spread of Christianity. The term is also used to refer to an extensive range of modern religions that are related to polytheistic Northern European worship.

Ásatrú (Asatru/Asatro)

The term Asatru, used to describe the indigenous religion of Europe, is old Norse and derives from two words, **Asa** which is one of the classes of Nordic Gods, and **tru** which means to be true, loyal or to be 'in troth' with. Hence, the term **Asatru** means to be true to the Aesir Gods. The term Asatru has become the dominant and prevailing term used to describe the indigenous Nordic religion, which refers to the Aesir deities. Other terms such as Odinism and Theodism have also been utilized. The former term tends to focus on the worship of the principal deity Odin, and the other, Theodism, being a more specific type of Asatru followed by the Anglo Saxons. Terms such as 'heathen' or 'pagan,' whilst often being a further title used in conjunction with Asatru, are broader terms generally referring to adherents of a polytheistic tradition often within a nature-based theological system. The term 'Forn Sed' is common in Scandinavian countries and means 'Old Way' and is considered as an alternative to the term Asatru.

The term **religion** needs to be utilized and considered in a broader context than traditionally perceived by most Westerners. The Nordic Religion is at its essence a tradition and an allegorical philosophy. Asatru is the cultural and allegorical native 'resource' of the Norse People. Only in this context is the term **religion** used in this book. Another common auxiliary and evolutionary hallmarks of religion, such as a codified dogma and a structured hierarchy with a priest class, is not a predeterminant feature of Asatru. The adherents of Asatru are free to practice in their ways but generally follow accepted traditional practices and propagate ancient allegorical philosophies.

They are free to make their interpretations of the tradition and are not bound to any ruling class, rather, only to their conscience and the collective conscience of their family or kin. Although Asatru has Priests and Priestesses, called Gothis, these people act as teachers and guides of the philosophy, **not** as hierarchical superpowers which dictate actions or act as intermediaries between the believer and deity. There is no ex-communication, no sin or salvation, nor does the religion of Asatru profess to lead the only pathway to enlightenment.

The Ásatrú adherents refer to themselves as Ásatrúar and prefer a reconstructionist approach in their practices. It is a community-based path, so any Ásatrúar acts for the good of the community. The community in this path is called "Kindred," and the congregation folk. The clergy are called goði and gyðja.

They often look on surviving texts for spiritual guidance. It is also the most well-known kind of modern practice of Norse paganism in the world at the moment.

Their central guidelines are based on Hávamál.

Anyone can join Ásatrú. However, only people from Iceland can be members of the Icelandic Norse Paganism organization, Ásatrúarfélagið.

The Ásatrúarfélagið has clerics who are called goði (priest) or gyðja (priestess; plural: goðar/gyðjur) each of whom is responsible for a goðorð, which is a congregation. Goðorð in the Old Norse religion was usually ascribed to geographic areas, but people had the freedom to choose their Goði. However, in Norse Paganism, there is no central authority or ahead of the faith to determine who is or isn't an adherent of the Norse faith. Just like the Old Norse, the rituals and practices of the Norse faith are as diverse today as they had been in the past. This allows Norse Pagans to research the faith on their own, practice, and celebrate according to their needs and the practices of their fellow local Norse Pagans.

Vanatru

This is a relatively new path. The name means "loyal to the Vanir," and it made its first appearance in the early 90s. It is very similar to Ásatrú but intended for people who feel closer to the Vanir than to the Æsir. It better serves those whose focus is on folk magic, witchcraft, divination, and nature.

Vanatru differs from Ásatrú when it comes to rituals. The deities in Vanatru are considered individuals, and each of them has specific rites and different ways with which one can communicate with them. Ásatrú, on the other hand, has similar ceremonies for all the deities.

Community is also quite important for Vanatru. This path is far less structured than Ásatrú.

Rökkatru

This is a term that was coined by an adherent named Abby Hellasdottir and means "loyal to the Rökkr." The Rökkr are deities considered darker, such as Loki and Hel and the Jötnar. They are more suited to people interested in the concepts of chaos, death, and the elements of cosmogenesis, ice, and fire.

Unlike the conditional equivalence of darkness and chaos with evil, the Rökkatru aren't evil or interested in evil deeds. Instead, they accept chaos and darkness as parts of the life cycle and deem them as parts of the cycle. This path doesn't mean that you are not allowed to honor other deities. However, it is important to understand their darker and more chaotic elements.

This is the path more closely linked to Norse Shamanism. It is mainly focused on the individual and their development and our connection to the Gods.

The term Rökkatru was later utilized by Raven Kaldera in several of his works and among the Northern Paganism group. This branch of Heathenry focuses mostly on the jotnar and their giant spiritual powers as well as the Norse pantheon's most chaotic deities in general. Several of the beings grouped as Rökkr are primordial notions and elemental wights like fire, ice, death, earth, and so on.

Heathens, on the whole, get their inspiration from first-hand lore (The Eddas, the Sagas, as well as some surviving ancient texts). To authentically reconstitute their practice, they also add an awareness of recent research, language analysis, and archaeological study. Nevertheless, in the recreated faith, unverified personal gnosis (UPG) plays a significant role, particularly In more diversified sects of Heathenry such as Rökkatru. Because there is so little recorded information on specific wights and deities, it's up to each person doing the ritual to gather as much information as possible and investigate the topic further.

Thursatru

Thursatru is a recent development in modern Norse Paganism and Heathenry. Its specific path appears to focus on being anti-Aesir, anti-Vanir, and pro-Thurses, a race of giants that are part of a branch of the jotunn family tree. Any concept that contradicts its established tradition and ideals is not considered Thursatru. The fundamentals of the known Thursian religion, called Thursatru or Thursatru Culture, differs from other branches of the Thursian religion, and there are interpretations as to why this is so. This tradition provides the major practitioner with the same knowledge foundation as members of other branches use, namely from the ancient books and other devotees, but it appears to split via the magnanimous Will of Thursian Powers. Whereas other traditions or forms of worship in Modern Norse Paganism are open to interpretation by the individual, this branch highlights the importance and significance of adhering to a rigid tradition rather than making adjustments and/or deletions to suit one's individual preferences to worship.

The fundamental essence of Thursatru is that it is a practical religio-sorcerous worshiping those old Norse titans known as thurses. Thursatru is a unique theological offspring of post-Norse religion, where Thursian gigantology and mythology are linked with anti-cosmic Gnosticism. In his 2010 book Gullveigarbók, Ekortu developed and presented the term **Thursatru** to distinguish his religious beliefs and practices from those of others. He authored the language used to describe its precise definition.

<u>Odinism</u>

Odinism is a Norse pantheon-based religion that praises Odin, Heimdallr, Freyr, Freyja, Heimdallr, as well as other Norse gods. Some believers associate Odinism with Asatru, while some do not. Furthermore, some followers associate their practice with Wodenism, or Wotanism, while others disagree. The religion is known as Forn Sed in Scandinavia.

Odinism is a recent resurgence of an old religion that was formerly and commonly accepted across northern Europe, particularly by the Norse. Modern Odinism is known by many different names and is sometimes referred to as Germanic Neopaganism by those who have studied the religion from an external perspective. In Heathenry, Satr is one of a variety of titles that have been used. For clarity's sake, the group's overarching umbrella term refers to these believers as Odinists. Whereas this religion has been around since it was created by Norse people, the modern rebirth of these ideas occurred during the early 20th Century. Paganism is, in some ways, the only global type of spirituality known to humankind, while Odinism is one section of the pagan group of religious beliefs within the Teutonic religious ideology.

Lokeans

A Lokean is anybody who reveres Loki and connects with him as their major deity in personal practice, regardless of whether they identify as Pagan or Heathen. In recent years, some individuals have started using the term Lokean as though it was a separate religion in its sense. Taking Loki out of his cultural context and focusing solely on him, to the extent of forgetting the presence of the other Norse Gods, effectively deprives him of his spiritual context and his natural role in the pantheon. It's crucial to understand what he's about and how he connects with the rest of the gods.

It's crucial to note that not everyone who identifies as Lokean also identifies as Rökkr. Most individuals who are members of Heathen culture do make these connections. Since several new Lokeans are giving up hope of being embraced by conventional Heathenry, perhaps related to encounters with Heathens who vehemently reject Loki-worshiping or the assumption that every heathen despises Loki, others have taken up this title.

There isn't any agreed-upon model of worshiping or an oath to take to become a Lokean. It's crucial to know the role and importance of a vow in current Heathenry or how they're expected to affect people in the physical and spiritual realm before throwing them around. In several Heathen cultures, oaths aren't taken lightly, and swearing an oath is seen as linking one's destiny, individual power, and honor to one's word. If other people are present for the oath, it is usually assumed that your luck and reputation are also at stake, as they are supposed to assist you in keeping your promise.

Making a vow to a god binds your fate, wealth, and existence to them, for better or worse. Individuals who breach their pledges are frowned upon in contemporary Heathenry, with some even suggesting that oath violators have no role in society or that they are cursed. Others believe that even if you violate your pledge to a deity for whichever reason, the gods might decide to take their retribution from you or possibly from everyone who observed the vow but did not hold people to the word, at their discretion.

Conclusion

Thank you for reading this book. The magic used by experienced practitioners is more complex than that of beginners. There are spells for different purposes too; ensure that you select the right one. You can also choose to perform a ritual for your spell or magic. Nobody knows how the rituals work, but it is believed that they stimulate the powers of nature and spirits for good purposes. Ceremonial magic and spells are often mixed with Norse Mythology and other magical arts to form powerful spells and rituals. Before you decide to embark on this spiritual journey, you should make sure you are ready for it.

You should look for local Norse Pagan groups or organizations if you feel like you want a community instead of pursuing a solitary path. Having a group will help you advance in your spiritual path and give you group practice.

As there is no dogma in Asatru, beliefs, and practices wildly vary. As Asatru encourages practitioners to develop their rituals and practices, no version is more accurate than others. The goal of Asatru isn't to indoctrinate or proselytize but to revive, reconstruct, and reimagine the ancient polytheistic faith of the Norse people.

Even though there is a severe lack of information on the worshiping practices, the information on Norse mythology that has survived is quite impressive. Norse mythology, which serves as the lore and tradition of Norse Paganism, is vast and colorful.

Ásatrú is perhaps one of the most well-known modern Norse Paganism practices. The little things we know about Old Norse religious practice include the fact that Norse chieftains also served as spiritual leaders or priests and that horse sacrifices were a part of pagan worship practices.

Rituals would take place in specific nature sites, like groves or lakes. There is evidence that houses could also be used for rituals, some of which were specifically built for cultic reasons. Despite Asatru's beliefs and rituals were considered to be unprecedented, the movement never compelled believers to follow them in order. It does, however, persuade people to focus on their actions because their life after death will be determined accordingly.

Today, Norse mythology retains a strong analogy on the creation of the earth and the establishment of order. Several religious adherents have converted to Norse Paganism and become Asatruars as a result of the beliefs and rituals. Indeed, as more awareness and freedom are gained, the hidden doors of Norse Paganism are being revealed and made available for religious believers to explore. Even if certain beliefs are slightly manipulated to fit the modern thinking pattern, the essence and authenticity of this domain remain intact.

Nowadays, Norse Paganism seems to be going through some sort of Renaissance. People who look into it are usually those who desire to reconnect with their roots or are looking for something ancestral and closer to their spirit.

Good luck.